# EGYPT

The Nile lifeline. Few countries in the world are characterized so dramatically by a single river as Egypt is. Below: Near Aswan, traditional single- or double-masted felucca sailing boats.

Snake charmers in Dendera: Day in and day out, tradition and modernity come together to create a new "moment of magic" in Egypt, a country rich in art, culture, myths and legends.

# ABOUT THIS BOOK

"You may have seen much of the planet, but if you haven't been to Egypt, you have not yet experienced the profundity of the world. Egypt is the alpha and the omega of all travel experiences." Travel writer Horst Krüger wrote this some fifty years ago and his claim is still entirely valid today. When contemplating the Land of the Nile, the mind instantly conjures up enticing images of a diver's paradise on the Red Sea, of remote desert oases and monasteries, and of the grand monuments of the pharaohs and of Islamic civilizations, from the pyramids and temples between El Gîza and Abu Simbel to Cairo's medieval mosques.

Another highlight of this country so rich in tradition is its people. The gracious character of the Egyptians is apparent at nearly every encounter. Whether you are ambling through the medieval alleyways and bazaars of Cairo's Old Town, exploring the Fellah villages in Upper Egypt and the Delta, or visiting ancient hermitages, the Bedouin tents of the Sinai or the air-conditioned office towers of Alexandria and Cairo, the Egyptians' cordial and peaceable demeanour and their profound piety leave as lasting an impression with visitors as the country's astounding historic relics and natural landscapes. Violence of the sort that occurred in the 1990s – occasionally also against foreign visitors – is fortunately not a common trait among Egyptians.

In this book we show you images of Egypt's breathtaking diversity, arranged by geographical regions. The map section allows you to orientate yourself, find sights of interest, get an overview of the routes that take you there, and set out on new journeys of discovery using the icons on the maps. The index, which links the picture section and the map pages, also provides you with Internet addresses for the most important sights. We hope you enjoy discovering Egypt.

Egypt extends from the Mediterranean Sea in the north and the Red Sea in the east to the Sahara in the south and west. Only four percent of the country (about 1,000,000 sq km/386,000 sq mi) can be used for agriculture. The majority of Egypt consists of sandy and rocky deserts that beset both banks of the Nile Valley and extend to the Sinai Peninsula. With roughly seventy million people, Egypt is one of the world's most densely populated countries.

# CONTENTS

Alexandria used to be called
"The Pearl of the Mediterranean".
At night you can still wander under
palm trees on the city's brightly
illuminated seaside promenade,
the Corniche.

The Nile Delta: Fellah farmers still
supply Egypt with much of its
grain, fruit and vegetables.
"Fellah" comes from the Arab word
"Fallah" (one who ploughs);
"falaha" means "working the soil".

# NILE DELTA AND MEDITERRANEAN COAST

Alexandria, once a venerated cosmopolitan metropolis, has indeed seen better days, but it is still worth exploring the city's glorious past. Situated on a spit of land between the Mediterranean and Lake Maryut on the north-western edge of the Nile Delta, you will be amazed by the numerous relics from ancient times. The rich green hinterland to the east – between Rosetta and Damietta – and the desert in the west are full of surprises, as is the shore towards Marsa Matruh.

Ancient relics here testify to the cult of Isis. Right: The goddess breastfeeding the boy Horus; a Ptolemaic glass tablet; Cleopatra as a magician; portrait of Cleopatra on a medallion. Below: A mosaic from the time of Ptolemy. Insets, bottom facing page: statues of Ptolemaic kings. Ptolemaic rule ended with Cleopatra VII (inset, top facing page), shown here in a painting by Frederick Stibbert and Benedetto Servolino (1869). The relief next to her is from the 1st century BC.

# AN IDEAL CITY ON THE MEDITERRANEAN

Alexander the Great could not have selected a better location when he decided to construct a port city on Egypt's Mediterranean coast. It has a low limestone shelf, a sizable freshwater inland lake, and a small island off the coast. Alexander had the latter connected with the mainland by a dam, creating the beloved twin-harbor where ships were able to dock no matter which way the wind was blowing. A network of canals was then constructed to connect the port and the lake with the Nile. Roads and residential housing were built in a chessboard pattern in order to expose them to the cool northerly winds. A number of parks and even a zoo were then added. At its peak, around the birth of Christ, the city covered an area of about 10 sq km (4 sq miles) and was home to nearly one million people. Its Museion was the most important research center in the world at that time, and its collection of 700,000 scrolls formed the world's largest library. In ancient times the city was even governed by one of the most legendary figures of all time: Cleopatra VII (69–30 BC). On the island of Pharos, which forms one end of the harbor, there once stood an enormous lighthouse (122 m/400 ft). The tower was destroyed by earthquakes in the early 1300s, but it is considered one of the Seven Wonders of the Ancient World.

The Qaitbay Citadel (below) was built in the 15th century where once the famous ancient lighthouse stood – on the former island of Pharos at the northern end of the Corniche promenade. A wide spit of land divides the port (right) into convenient eastern and western basins.

## Alexandria (1)

The harbor in Alexandria, where once the Pharos lighthouse stood, is dominated by the Ottoman Qaitbay Citadel. The district of Bahari extends toward the city and has an Oriental feel with narrow alleyways, busy bazaars and several large mosques. On its western edge is the Ras el-Tin Palace. Its counterpoint is the Midan al-Tahrir square, the heart of modern Alexandria in the 19th century, surrounded by residential homes, department stores, churches and foreign consulates. The most important monuments of the ancient world are the Roman baths, the Kom el-Dikka amphitheater, the early Ptolemaic tombs of Anfushi, the Kom ash-Shuqqafa catacombs and the famous, 27-m-high (88-ft) "Pompey's Pillar", which is guarded by two sphinxes. The Greco-Roman Museum is a treasure trove of relics from the period between 300 BC and AD 300.

Below: A magnificent façade on the Corniche and an alleyway in the old town. Facing page, from top: The Rialto Cinema; Brazilian Coffee Store; the train station. Right: A sunset silhouette with the city's minarets; Abu al-Abbas al-Mursi Mosque; the Mohamed Ali Sayed Darwish Theater.

## Alexandria (2)

Today, Alexandria is home to more than six million people, and more than forty percent of Egypt's industry is here. The view of the skyline is sobering, and the air is heavy with smog, but that reality has only minimal impact on the mythical status of the city. In 1900, Alexandria was still one of the eastern Mediterranean's most cosmopolitan centers, home to wealthy Greeks and Syrian Lebanese communities, Armenian and Italian artisans, adventurous Englishmen, and enterprising Jews seeking fortunes in the cotton trade. Many an eclectic façade along the Corniche, in the elegant districts of Moharrem Bey and Montazah, still bear witness to that heyday. In some of the cafés and art-deco cinema houses you can imagine rubbing shoulders with the characters from the *Alexandria Quarte*, Lawrence Durrell's immortal tetralogy of novels.

Below and facing page: Postmodernism meets antiquity, symbolically united in the multilingual carvings on the wall of the Bibliotheca Alexandrina. Right: Restorers at work preserving the valuable scriptures in the library (on the left a royal decree from Cleopatra's time).

# A MILESTONE OF POSTMODERN ARCHITECTURE

Just two or three generations ago, Egypt's legendary port town was still romantically described as the "Pearl of the Mediterranean". Its allure has faded slightly since then, but two projects are set to re-establish Alexandria as an intellectual and cultural center, and as a hub of knowledge in the Arab, African and Mediterranean worlds: Senghor University, founded in 1990, and the new "Bibliotheca Alexandrina". The latter, a milestone of postmodern architecture designed by an international team of architects under Norwegian direction, finally opened in 2002 after lengthy delays. It houses nearly 4.5 million books. Will it ever be able to hold a candle to its ancient predecessor, which stood on the very same site? Built by Ptolemy I at the beginning of the 3rd century BC, it had been the most important library of the ancient world, and of vital importance in disseminating Greek knowledge and further developing the sciences. It was indeed no accident that, in this environment, Aristarchus first devised a heliocentric model of the world; that Archimedes developed his screw as well as the block and tackle pulley system; that Eratosthenes of Cyrene calculated the Earth's circumference; that Euclid wrote his textbook of geometry; and that Ptolemy drafted the foundations of astronomy.

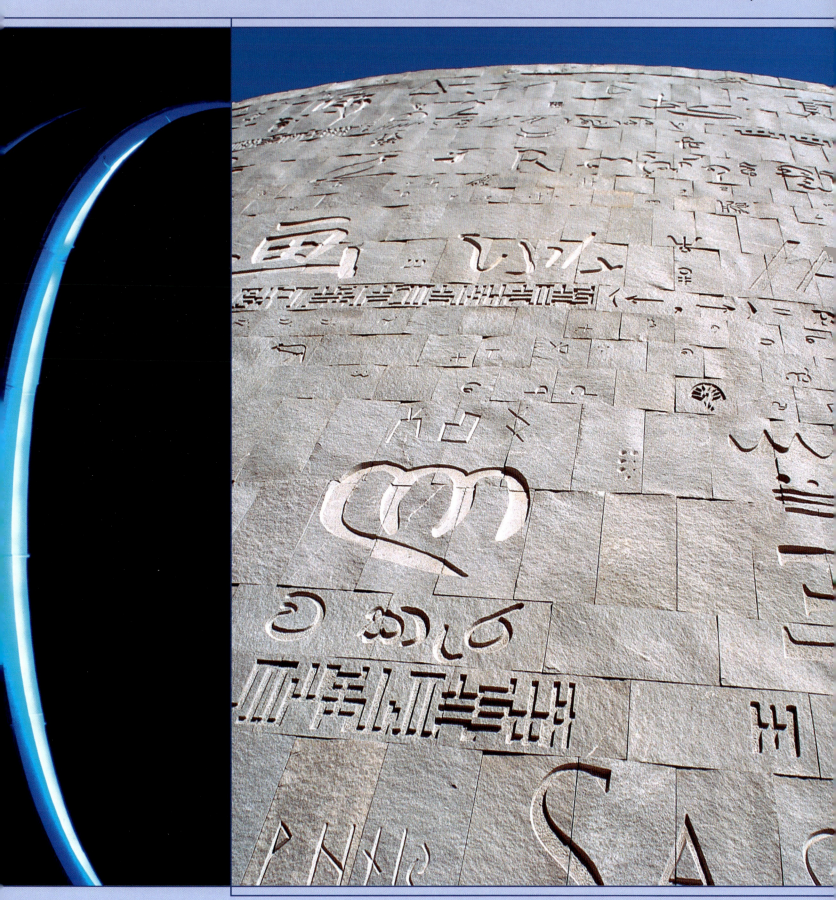

Below: North of Cairo, the Nile flows into the Mediterranean in two large tributaries, the entire delta covering roughly 24,000 sq km (9,264 sq miles). Right: Near Rosetta (Rashid), a stone was discovered whose trilingual inscriptions finally made it possible to decipher ancient hieroglyphics.

## Nile Delta

There are no grand temples or tombs here. Hotels and souvenir shops are extremely rare. In the Nile Delta, modest everyday farming sets the tone. Charming but unspectacular, the mud huts and small, parcelled fields of rice, cotton and an array of vegetables are confined by tidy, narrow drainage ditches. Yet the flat, evergreen floodplains are not entirely devoid of attractions. In the east, for example, are the ruins of the Ptolemaic metro-polis of Tanis. At the mouth of the Nile's eastern branch, on the shores of Lake Manzala, is the port town of Damietta, long important as a transhipment point and a center for the textile industry. At the end of the Nile's western branch is the town of Rosetta, made famous by the Rosetta Stone, which helped Jean-François Champollion (1790–1832) decipher ancient Egyptian hieroglyphics.

Roughly three-quarters of Egyptians consider themselves the descendants of indigeonous rural farming people, or Fellahs, who are thought to be direct descendants of Pharaonic Egypt and place great value on upholding the ancient traditions of their forefathers.

# THE FELLAHS: FARMING LIFE ON THE NILE

The life-giving Nile has a profound impact on the mentality and lifestyle of the farmers, or Fellahs, who live on its banks. Indeed, the river's rise and fall, the germination and cultivation of the seeds, the harvest, and the constant rhythm of nature have defined the collective soul of the people here for milennia. The certainty of the inevitable, the confidence instilled by this rhythm, and the unswerving tranquility and cheerfulness are still tangible today in both villages and larger towns on the delta. Numerous waves of immigrants, from the Hyksos, Nubians and Assyrians to the Persians, Greeks and Romans as well as the Arabs and the Turks have invaded and taken control of the Nile Delta. They have even blended in with the local population to a certain extent. And yet the people on the Nile have proven themselves resilient not only to centuries of invasion, but also to political and social upheaval. Traditionally, they have met foreigners with tolerance and have preferred integration to rejection. Thomas Mann remarked of a "fundamentally idiosyncratic, omniscient divine spirit that creates man and creature in its image" here. Viennese cultural historian Egon Friedell wrote of the "age-old rhythm of the vegetative metabolism" in the region, of the "andante in their pace of life".

Below: The many depictions of Ramses (in giant statues, reliefs, and sarcophagi) led to the belief that a Ramses city existed within the city of Tanis. Right: Masks of kings Sheshonk and Amenemope, entombed in Tanis, and a sphinx. Facing page: Inside the tomb of King Osorkon II.

## Tanis

For a long time, experts believed that the ruins of Tanis – roughly thirty minutes north of Qantir – were the remains of the former center of Ramses' empire. Richard Lepsius and Auguste Mariette, two renowned Egyptologists, even began a lively Franco-German debate on the subject as early as the mid-19th century. Over time, however, it has come to light that the city of Tanis was built during a dynasty that came roughly 200 years after that of Ramses. The reason for the confusion was that they had brought stones and statues from Pi-Ramesse and "re-used" them here. Ultimately, this fact does not diminish the impact of these vast ruins, with imposing walls, columns, and tombs as well as colossal statues and obelisks. Tanis is now supervised mostly by French archaeologists and has been accessible to tourists for some time.

Discoveries such as the stele of Ramses II (below) make any archaeologist's heart race with excitement. Facing page: The Nile Delta at Qantir; excavation sites at Pi-Ramesse (top, center) and Tell el-Dab'a. Right: A well of Ramses II; archaeologists in Pi-Ramesse.

## Pi-Ramesse, Tell el-Dab'a

Over the last twenty years, north of the Fellah village of Qantir in the eastern Nile Delta, German archaeologists have managed to unearth the remains of Pi-Ramesse ("The House of Ramses"), birthplace of the mighty Ramses II. In the 13th century BC, this "King of Kings" moved the seat of government here from Memphis. In an area roughly 30 sq km (12 sq miles) in size, the remains of workshops and stables have provided valuable insights into the everyday life of ancient Egyptians. Nearby, at Tell el-Dab'a, Austrian colleagues have excavated the remains of the Hyksos capital of Avaris. Extensive Minoan frescoes, ceramics and jewellery here provide testimony to the cultural diversity of the peoples and cultures of the eastern Nile Delta and show the close links that existed between this region and the Levant, especially Crete.

The Wadi el-Natrûn (Natron Valley) was named after the natron that was harvested here already in the days of the pharaohs. It lies in a desert depression that is approximately 22 m (24 yds) below sea level. You can visit four of originally fifty Coptic monasteries here.

## The Monasteries of Wadi el-Natrûn

South-east of the main road, about halfway between Alexandria and Cairo, is the 50-km-long (30-miles) Wadi el-Natrûn monastery complex. This desolate strip of land also features salt lakes that dry out in summer and were once the source of natron salt for the embalmers of the pharaohs. The salt helped draw water from the mummified corpses. Since the 4th century, the area has been a center for Christian monks. At its peak, more than fifty monasteries here accommodated nearly 50,000 men. Four of these monasteries – Deir el-Baramus, Deir Abu Makar, Deir es-Suriani and Deir Anba Bishoi – are still inhabited today. Behind their mighty walls are impressive monastic facilities and you can visit churches that are more than 1,000 years old, with original frescoes, priceless pictographs and iconostases carved from wood and ivory.

"The Copts … are very important as partners and mediators between the West and Islam. We understand the language … and we are happy to act as mediators and attempt to facilitate cooperation," says Anba Damian, Coptic Orthodox Bishop of Germany.

# THE COPTS: "CHURCH OF THE MARTYRS"

Today, the term "Copt", which originally just meant "Egyptian", is used to describe Christians in Egypt. The Copts regard themselves as the cultural descendants of the oldest Christian community outside of Palestine, and they proudly point out that they once hosted the Holy Family for three years in Egypt. Approximately eight million Christians live in this predominantly Muslim country on the Nile, and since ancient times the Copts have produced a disproportionate part of the country's elite. As a result, the Copts were often persecuted, which is why people also speak of the "Church of the Martyrs". Traditionally, they settled in Middle Egypt, between El-Minia and Kena, but also had communities in Cairo and Alexandria. In the Middle Ages, their language was suppressed by Arabic, surviving mainly in liturgy. Mark the Evangelist originally founded the Coptic Orthodox Church as early as the 1st century AD. Considered the cradle of Christian Monasticism, Copts proselytized among Nubians and Ethiopians, among others, and allegedly spread the word of Christianity as far afield as Ireland. Its followers fervently revere the Crucifix and the Holy Virgin. The head of the church is his Grace Anba Shenuda III, the "Pope and Patriarch of Alexandria", who is said to be the 117th successor of St Mark.

Discovered in 1905, the ruins of churches, monasteries and pilgrim accommodations in Abu Mena are now a UNESCO World Heritage Site in Danger. They are under threat from rising ground water. Right: Marsa Matruh and a stretch of beach known as "Cleopatra's Bath".

## Abu Mena to Marsa Matruh

About 50 km (30 miles) south-west of Alexandria are the ruins of Egypt's largest early Christian settlement. When the soldier and future saint, Menas, died a martyr's death in 296 AD, his final resting place became a pilgrimage site. It quickly grew into a sizable community, which ultimately had its heyday from the 5th to the 7th centuries. Recognizable among the archaeological remains are bath complexes, pilgrim hostelries, a mona-stery and several churches. Some stretches of the coastline to the west have since been heavily developed with holiday villas, but the beaches are still stunning. The most attractive bay, Agiba – "the wonderful" – is located near Marsa Matruh, the administrative center of this vast province (with only 220,000 inhabitants), that extends west from Alexandria more than 500 km (310 miles) to the border with Libya.

Fancy a hookah? Well, if you're lucky you may just be able to enjoy one during the evening rush hour from one of the many hookah vendors plying the busy streets of the capital.

Cairo is also known as the "City of a Thousand Minarets". Below: The towers of the 14th-century Sultan Hassan Mosque and those of the Er Rifai Mosque next to it, dating from 1912.

# CAIRO

"He who hasn't seen Cairo has not seen the world," says the tale of the Arabian Nights. Today, nearly one in four of the seventy million people in Egypt live here, Africa's largest city. The glitter of the metropolis on the Nile may have faded a little since the days of Scheherazade, but Cairo is much more than just the undisputed political, intellectual and economic center of the country. It is the epitome of the Western vision of an "Oriental" city and fascinates visitors to this day.

Over ninety percent of Egyptians are Sunni Muslims, and their mosques define the cityscape. Below: The Ibn Tulun Mosque, completed in 879. Facing page: The Sultan Qaitbay Mosque, completed in 1474. Right: The courtyard of the Amr Ibn El-As Mosque, founded in 641.

## The Islamic Old Town

Al Qahirah (the "Triumphant") – a name that would later be distorted by Italian merchants to become Cairo – was founded in the year 969 by the Fatimid caliphs, Shiite rulers, near the ancient Arabic settlement of Fustat, and was initially a palace complex. It was Saladin, the famous founder of the Ayyubid Dynasty, who first opened the royal enclosure to ordinary citizens. Over the years, sultans, princes and viziers all tried to outdo each other as architects of the thoroughfare – today's Sharia Al-Mu'izz Li-Din – which was then known as Qasaba. UNESCO has listed more than 600 monuments in the Old Town – and they are in dire need of protection. The grand mosques and mausoleums, madrassas and manors, hospitals and steam baths, wells and caravanserais are all suffering from decay caused by air pollution and sewage issues.

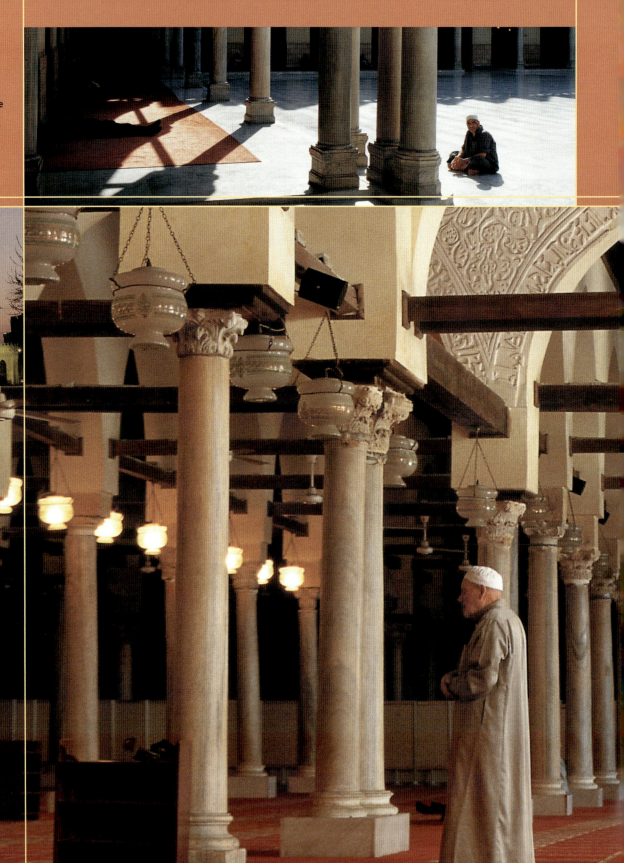

Construction of the Al-Azhar Mosque began as early as 970. Since 989, it has housed the University of Islamic Law and Arabic Language. The chancellor of this world center of Sunni tradition is also the highest religious authority in Egypt.

# AL-AZHAR: SPIRITUAL CENTER OF THE ARAB WORLD

At the heart of the Old Town are the Al-Azhar Mosque and University. They were named after Fatima, the Prophet's daughter, who is said to have been so beautiful that she was given the epithet al-Zahra ("the Most Flourishing and Shining"). For more than 1,000 years, the intricate complex of buildings, comprising five minarets, a place of worship, a madrassa (Koranic school) and student residences has long been the intellectual center and focal point of power for the Arab and Muslim world, as well as a center of education and identity. It is governed by the ulama and headed by the Grand Imam, the supreme guardian over fundamental and legal questions for Sunni Muslims. He enjoys global recognition among the faithful. In Egypt, Al-Azhar spearheads the education of the next generation of theologians through twenty of its own colleges and 2,000 secondary schools – all parallel to the state's system. Typically, a muted bustle prevails in the inner courtyard, which is surrounded by alabaster columns. The adjoining prayer hall once served as a lecture hall and on occasion you can still observe traditional open sessions among the forest of 375 pillars. Due to the sheer numbers, however, many of the faculties – with roughly 150,000 students – have been relocated elsewhere.

Cairo's Old Town is a feast for the senses. Where else would you find an open-air butcher shop? And where else do the spices and freshly baked bread smell as wonderfully as here? Where could the artisans' hammering mingle with the voices of story-tellers and the bleating of camels?

# Gamaliya and Ghuriya

Gamaliya and Ghuriya, the two central districts of the Old Town, are home not only to the late Naguib Mahfouz, winner of the Nobel Prize for Literature, but many of his protagonists as well. On the north side, the districts extend beyond the town wall, which dates back to Saladin's days and has two gates, the Bab el-Futuh and Bab el-Nasr. On the south side they go beyond the twin towers of Bab Zuwayla toward the Citadel. A stroll through the alleyways reveals a fascinating world of labyrinthine bazaars, dingy workshops and caravanserais, market stalls and ancient mosques. The lasting images here are of a dense jumble of housewives doing their daily shopping, of children playing in the streets, of porters, traders and idlers; of donkey, hand and horse carts, of cyclists and of incessantly honking car horns.

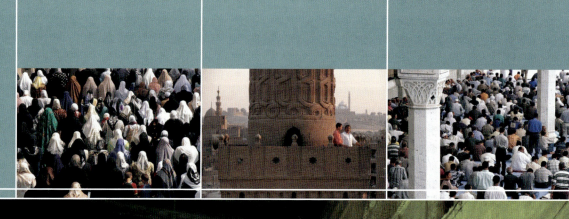

"O ye who believed and were God-fearing will receive the glad tidings of paradise, in life and in the afterlife," promises the Koran. Below: Morning prayers at the Ibn Tulun Mosque. Facing page and right: The faithful in Cairo's Islamic quarter.

# "ALLAHU AKBAR" AND MUSLIM PRAYER

"Allah is great! ... there is no god but Allah ... and Mohammed is His Prophet ..." These are the words cried out by the mosque muezzin to summon the faithful to prayer – one of the five pillars of Islam. Prayer provides daily structure for Muslims, and helps direct their attention away from earthly distractions and towards the reason for their existence. A precondition for prayer is ritual purification. As such, ablutions immediately precede prayers. In the mosque, the faithful stand in rows, facing Mecca. Men and women are strictly segregated. To pray, first both hands are lifted up and several professions of faith are spoken along with some passages (Suras) from the Koran. This is followed by the person bending at the waist, while repeatedly reciting "Allahu Akbar" (Allah is great) and other words of praise. After this, while reciting further supplications, the praying Muslim drops to a prostrate position as a sign of devotion, touching the floor with his toes, knees, palms of the hands and forehead. Each prayer consists of several such cycles of movement, repeated twice or four times depending on the time of day. Finally, the pious Muslim says the so-called prayer of testimony, and wishes other devotees that the "peace and mercy of Allah be unto you".

What are you after? Khan el-Khalili most likely has it: from antiques (below) or a charming fez to spices and jewelry (right). And for those looking for something to quench their Cairo thirst, street vendors (facing page) offer refreshments such as chilled lime juice.

# Souk Khan el-Khalili

Bordered by Muski Street and the Hussein Mosque, Khan el-Khalili – Cairo's great souk or market – attracts visitors like a giant magnet. This traditional hub of commerce takes its name from a Mamluk stableman who, more than 600 years ago, had an extensive trading complex built here. The area near the bazaar was once the spice market where merchants from southern Arabia, Persia and India traded their exotic scented wares.

Today, the range of goods for sale consists first and foremost of alabaster sphinxes, upholstered leather pouffes, brass plates and similar knick-knacks for the credit-card-wielding tourists from overseas. At best, locals will buy a bit of jewelry here. As far as atmosphere is concerned, the labyrinth of narrow and largely covered alleyways with teeming crowds still offers that authentic bazaar feel.

"In the clouds of my hookah, the bud of buds ripens [...] Foggy significances and obligations / drift away in the noise and dust of the street / Of planning, petitioning, undertaking / only a faint scheming remains in the heart." Franz Werfel from *At the Cairo Coffeehouse*.

# COFFEEHOUSES: A REFUGE FOR MEN

A regular component of many early travel accounts from Cairo was the description of a classic Cairo coffeehouse. From Gérard de Nerval to Gustave Flaubert, almost all foreign visitors to Egypt have extolled the unique magic, the quintessence of the Oriental mentality and the joie de vivre of these establishments. Indeed, it can be said that the Arabian Nights atmosphere has survived all attempts at modernization. They are still the places where men – exclusively men – indulge themselves with great fervor in the art of doing nothing. The main activity – now as then – is the simple yet vital enjoyment of a coffee or tea, a seemingly inalienable everyday ritual for locals here. Sugar is also an indispensable ingredient for Cairoans, unlike the Bedouins who prefer their bitter elixir spiced only with cardamom. You have the choice between "qahwa sada" (strong black), "wasat" (medium) and "arriha" (lightly sweetened). The perfect complement is naturally the hookah (narghilè), whose soothing sound and tobacco aroma are a delight for smokers. The men of Cairo often cluster around the coffeehouse table to play cards, dominoes or backgammon (tawla). To get away from the very sociable crowds, patrons can at least retreat inwardly with their misbaha (the 33-bead prayer string).

It is the white walls that gave the Mohammed Ali Mosque its other name – the Alabaster Mosque. Mohammed Ali (1769–1849), who is revered as the founder of modern Egypt, lies buried in the western corner of the domed Byzantine structure.

# Mohammed Ali Mosque

Among Cairo's many mosques, a good number of them stand out for their architecture as well as their atmosphere. The Ibn Tulun Mosque, for example, has a delightfully simple courtyard dating back more than 1,000 years, and its minaret with a helical outer staircase is inspired by Iraqi models. Other examples are the Mosque of the Mamluk Sultan Hassan and, immediately opposite, the equally colossal Al-Rifai Mosque, nearly 500 years younger. Another impressive monument, in both senses, is the Mohammed Ali Mosque (1824–57) with its pencil minarets and mighty vaulted dome. Defining the silhouette of the old town, it perches high on the Citadel hill. The fortress complex to which it belongs was mostly built during the time of Saladin (12th century) and even served as a military base well into the 1980s.

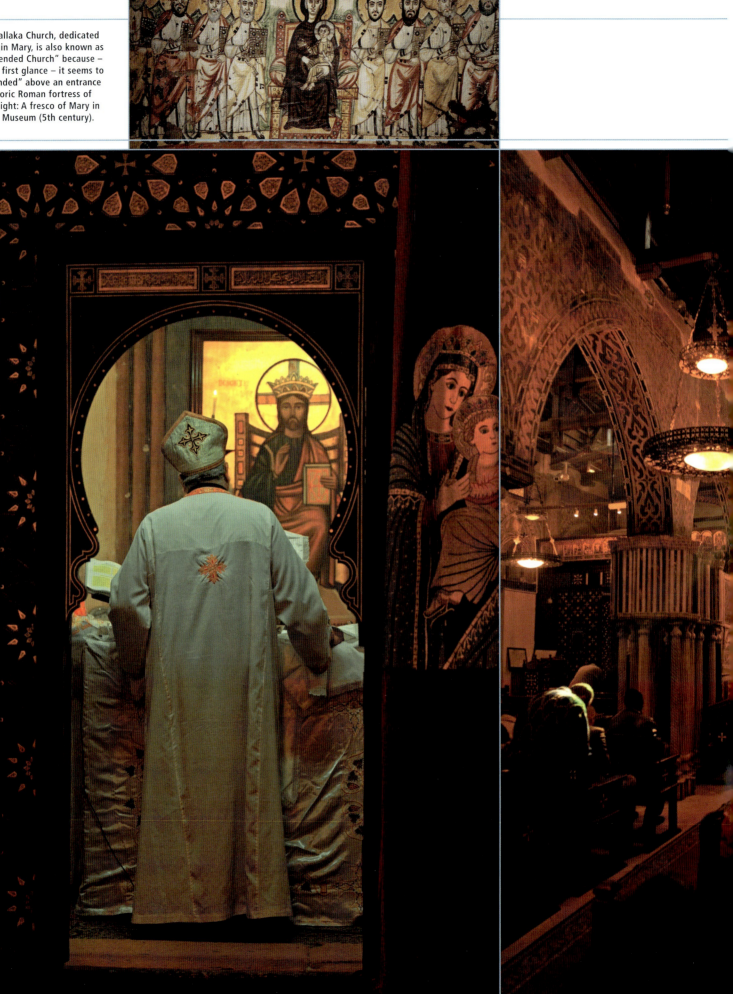

The Al-Moallaka Church, dedicated to the Virgin Mary, is also known as "The Suspended Church" because – at least at first glance – it seems to be "suspended" above an entrance to the historic Roman fortress of Babylon. Right: A fresco of Mary in the Coptic Museum (5th century).

## Old Cairo – the Coptic Quarter

Old Cairo, a district to the south of the Islamic Old Town on the Nile, is predominantly a Coptic area and enjoys 2,000 years of history. A Roman fortress called Babylon dominated shipping lanes on the river here back in the time of the emperors Hadrian and Trajan. And in the year 642, the Islamic conqueror Amr Ibn El-As set up an encampment here that later became the first Arabic capital of Egypt. Inside the Ben Ezra Synagogue, a unique treasure was discovered in a genizah, or secret hiding place for scriptures: more than 250,000 book fragments and certificates documenting in great detail the everyday life and commercial transactions of local Jewish traders over a period of 800 years. Also noteworthy is the Coptic Al-Moallaka Church, "The Suspended Church", with its more than 100 icons, some of which are over 1,000 years old.

Cairo in transition: High-rises, neon advertising and mobile phones are all part of daily life here now. Even the late Naguib Mahfouz (1911–2006), winner of the Nobel Prize for Literature, acknowledged the rapid change: "You've come because of the Nobel Prize? But that was yesterday!"

# MODERN CAIRO

In about 1900, Cairo had a population of roughly 500,000. Since then, the population has grown more than thirtyfold. In districts such as Shubra, or around the Bab al-Shariah gate, nearly 400,000 people are packed into each square mile of space. But if you thought that this situation was beyond the pale you would be underestimating the Egyptian spirit of improvisation and renewal. Living conditions are still precarious – the traffic is insane, the air can be cut with a knife, the noise is unnerving and the density extreme – but recently the city's infrastructure has made considerable progress. Telecommunications have greatly improved, a metro is under construction, and electricity and sewage facilities are more reliable. In addition, a dynamic middle class has emerged, and they are enjoying many Western comforts in new apartment districts such as Dokki, Maadi or Mohandessin. Since the middle of the 1980s, radio and TV regularly broadcast information on family planning, and a dense network of well-equipped clinics has been established where free contraception is available after a consultation with a doctor. Even Islamic clerics have relaxed their attitudes and in theory support the use of birth control. The result: in 1986, Egypt's population grew by 2.8 percent; in 2005 only by 1.8 percent.

By taxi through the back alleys and side streets of Cairo. Whether you're on a shopping spree, heading to a cultural event or simply out for a stroll, for Naguib Mahfouz these labyrinthine streets are "the symbol of the whole world". Right: Backstage at the Cairo Opera.

## Esbekiya – Colonial Cairo

Around 1870, Khedive Ismail, who was influential in the Europeanization of Egypt, made the area north-east of Tahrir Square (known as Esbekiya) the modern heart of the metropolis. In deliberate contrast to the Islamic Old Town, he established a spacious garden of pleasures here, with luxurious coffeehouses, hotels, a theater and an opera house. Wide boulevards radiate from generous plazas, following the model of Paris. Many architectural reminders from this period of radical Westernization have been preserved including monumental residential and office blocks with magnificent façades and portals that contain Art Nouveau, Art Deco, neoclassicist and neobaroque nuances. An especially opulent example is Midan Talaat Harb Square, named after the leading industrial tycoon of the 1930s. The "Groppi", once Cairo's most famous café, is also still there.

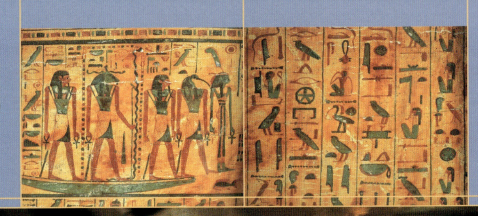

The principal attractions at the Egyptian Museum are the death masks of the ancient Egyptian kings (pharaohs). Below: The golden mask of Tutankhamun. Also part of the museum is a mummy conservation workshop (facing page, bottom). Right: The lid of Queen Nesikhonsu's coffin. Facing page, center: Detail of the Canopic chest, carved from gilded wood, which held Tutankhamun's mummified entrails.

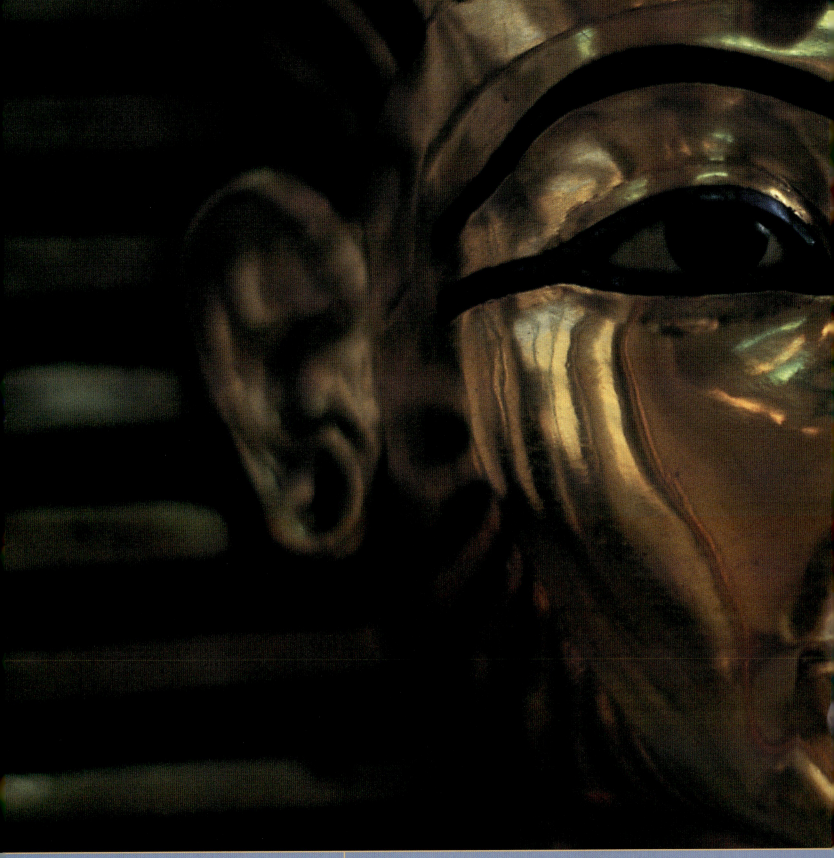

# THE EGYPTIAN MUSEUM: HERITAGE OF THE PHARAOHS

One of the first destinations for any new-comer will be Tahrir Square and the Egyptian Museum. There is hardly another place that evokes the singularity of this country quite so intensely. Three thousand years and 31 dynasties – from King Narmer, the first pharaoh, right up to the last rulers of the Late Period – astound visitors in over 50 rooms of this building, which is more than 100 years old. Thousands of steles, reliefs and sarcophagi, jewelry, small houses, ship models and other sacrificial offerings absolutely command appreciation. Most impressive, however, are the countless statues of gods in the form of humans or animals, the mummy of the pharaoh Tutankhamun and the treasures discovered in his burial chamber by Howard Carter in the Valley of the Kings in 1922. Construction of a new, ultramodern museum has been discussed for years, a veritable world center for Egyptology at the edge of the desert near El Gîza. And it is an understandable plan from an archaeologist's or conservationist's perspective: With more than 70,000 exhibits, the current building is as crowded as the country whose history it documents. But it will be nearly impossible to recreate the atmosphere and exhibition techniques of the current neoclassical building designed by Marcel Dourgnon.

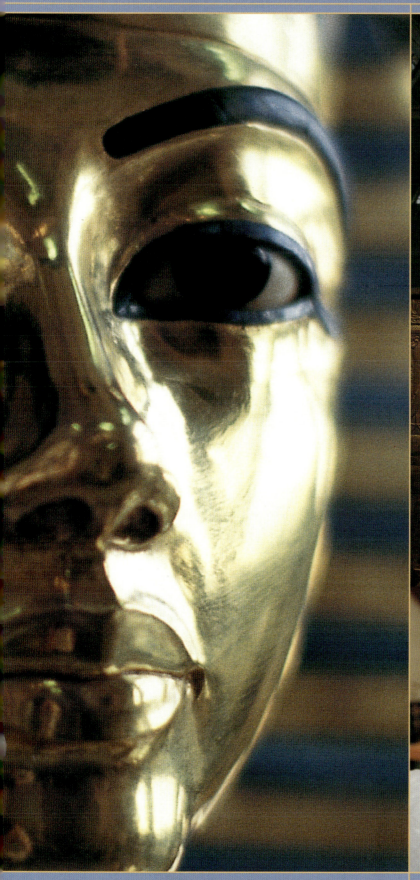

The pyramids of El Giza are the only Wonder of the Ancient World to have survived until the present day. "Men fear time, but time fears the pyramids," wrote Scheherazade in the Arabian Nights.

A sphinx, a half-human, half-lion guardian depicting the Sun God and measuring more than 70 m (77 yds) long and roughly 20 m (66 ft) high, squats on a plateau in front of Khafre's Pyramid squats.

# FROM EL GIZA TO EL FAIYÛM

There are some 100 pyramids south of Cairo on the west bank of the Nile. They were erected over the course of 1,000 years as the final resting places of the pharaohs, or kings. The original prototype was the step pyramid of Saqqara, which was built around the year 2550 BC. The Great Pyramid (or Pyramid of Khufu) is the largest of them. It was also the tallest structure in the world until the Eiffel Tower was completed. A visit to at least the most important of these ancient wonders is a must for any traveler.

Monumental burial chambers were once the expression of power. The Solar Barque, excavated on the east side of the Great Pyramid (facing page), took the embalmed king into the afterlife. Right: At night, a sound and light show creates an impressive spectacle of the pyramids.

## The Pyramids of El Giza

Although the provincial capital of El Giza physically merged with nearby Cairo long ago, it is fully in charge of its own administration. With more than 2.5 million inhabitants, the city enjoys world fame thanks to its three pyramids: the tombs of Khufu, his son Khafre and his grandson Menkaure. At an original height of more than 143 m (469 ft) (today it measures 136 m (446 ft)), the Great Pyramid is the tallest of the three. The middle Khufu Pyramid appears to be taller when seen from a distance, but that is due to its slightly elevated position and the partial original casing at the tip. The Great Pyramid consists of about 2.5 million blocks of rock weighing 2,500 kg (5,513 lbs) each. During his Egyptian campaign in the year 1798, Napoleon's engineers calculated that there were enough blocks to build a 3-m-high (10-ft) wall all the way around France.

In Memphis, essentially only the colossal limestone figure of Pharaoh Ramses II (below) and the giant alabaster sphinx (right, center) have survived. Right: The step pyramid of Saqqara. Far right: A relief from the tomb of Mereruka, a top-ranking official and priest.

## Memphis, Saqqara

Very little remains of ancient Memphis, the capital of the Old Kingdom about 20 km (12 miles) south of El Giza. Its roots go back to the fifth millennium BC, and it remained an important strategic outpost until Greco-Roman times. The most important remains here are an alabaster sphinx and the colossal figure of the reclining Ramses II. Also very impressive is the old cemetery of Memphis, Saqqara, ancient Egypt's largest necropolis.

At the heart of the extensive complex is the burial precinct of King Djoser, whose roughly 4,600-year-old step pyramid is considered the oldest stone structure in human history. With their attractive relief pictures, the numerous mastabas (tombs) offer superb insight into the everyday life of top-ranking officials as well as farmers, artisans and fishermen. They also depict the flora and fauna of the day.

These paintings, by contemporaries of Napoleon during his invasion of Egypt, depict a hero, graciously pardoning the "Rebels of Cairo" (below), storming into a mosque on horseback (facing page) and riding before his troops into battle on the Nile and near the pyramids (right).

# FORCED MODERNITY: NAPOLEON IN EGYPT

Napoleon's expedition in Egypt provided impetus for the first advance of Christian Europe into the Muslim world. In 1798, the French emperor arrived on the Egyptian coast with an entire navy, intending to blockade the route to India against his archenemy, the British. He stormed Alexandria, vanquished the army of the Mam-luks near the pyramids and ultimately occupied Cairo. However, just a few days later, the British, under the command of Admiral Nelson, sank the entire French fleet in Abū Qīr Bay. In reality, Napoleon foresaw his military defeat here, even at the beginning of 1799. Having returned that same year to France, the Corsican general was followed two years later by his army after a comprehensive trouncing. But while the rivalry with England took center stage for Napoleon, his transport ships not only carried cannons and soldiers but also about 200 engineers and scholars, a sizeable library, and technical and scientific instruments. In the true spirit of the Enlightenment, the French subsequently founded an institute in Cairo dedicated to "the systematic study of the Nile country and its Pharaonic inheritance". The result was a 24-volume *Description de l'Egypte*, which started a virtual mania in Europe for all things Egyptian, and indeed all things Oriental.

"Snofru's Apparition" is the name given to the Red Pyramid (below left) by the ancient Egyptians. Right: The Bent Pyramid. Facing page: This figure found in Dahshur and carved from cedar wood represents a Nubian courtesan. It is 65 cm (26 in) tall.

## Dahshur

The burial field of Dahshur is located on the left bank of the Nile a few miles south of Saqqara. Its main attractions are the Bent Pyramid and the Red Pyramid. Both were built more than 4,500 years ago by King Snofru. The former, roughly 105 m (345 ft) high, can only be viewed from outside. Its name comes from its two angles of inclination: in the lower part fifty-five degrees, and in the upper part only forty-three degrees.

It is theorized that the first proved too steep once half the structure had been erected and the outer blocks threatened to slip. It was thus decided to continue construction at a shallower angle. The Red Pyramid, named for the hue of its stone blocks, reaches a height of 101 m (331 9 ft). It is fully open to the public, right down to its innermost burial chamber, and is the oldest structure to have been built in a pure pyramid shape.

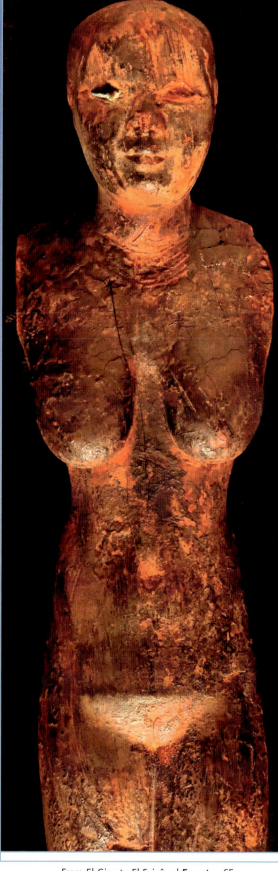

Below: Fossils of the now extinct "archaeoceti", or original, whale have been found here in Wadi Al-Hitan. It was a predecessor to the whales that now ply our oceans. Right: The Arabic name El Faiyûm means "lakelands". Right: Some scenes of Qarun Lake.

## El Faiyûm Oasis, Wadi Al-Hitan

The oasis landscape of El Faiyûm, some 90 km (56 miles) south of Cairo, covers an area just under 1,800 sq km (695 sq miles) making it Egypt's second-largest agricultural zone after the Nile Delta. Home to more than two million people, it is considered Cairo's bread basket. The capital, Medinet El Faiyûm, has a population of more than 250,000. The marshes in this fertile province had already been drained during the time of the pha-

raohs using dykes and canals, and today the region is irrigated with Nile water via the Yusuf Canal. Reminders of the area's heyday more than 4,000 years ago are the pyramids of Sesostris II (near El-Lâhûn) and Amenemhat III (near Hawara). In the northwest of the oasis basin is Qarun Lake, a slightly saline lake with abundant fish. Also worth seeing is the Wadi Al-Hitan ("Valley of the Whales"), famous for its petrified skeletons.

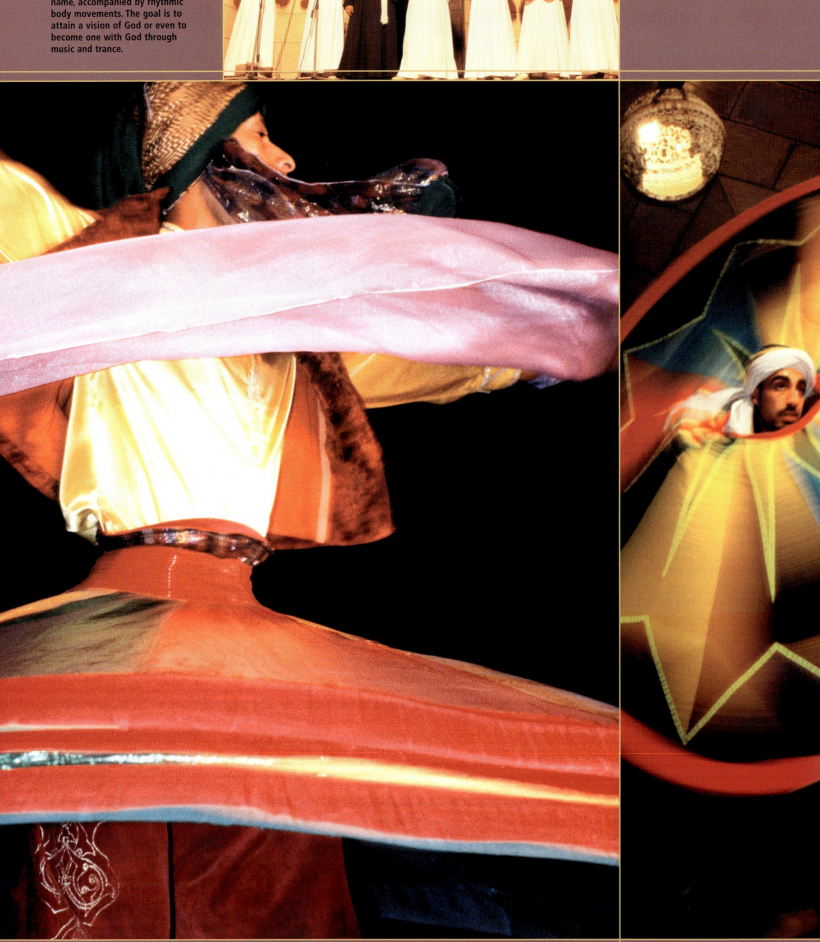

Typical of this mystical form of Islam, Sufis "worship" God through virtually endless repetition of God's name, accompanied by rhythmic body movements. The goal is to attain a vision of God or even to become one with God through music and trance.

# SUFISM – THE OTHER ISLAM

Sufism is a more mystical dimension of Islam and is widespread in Egypt. Its followers are members of fraternities that meet regularly in order to reach a higher level of consciousness through song, dance and prayer. For their predecessors – named Sufi for the woollen habits they wore (from Arabic "sûf" for wool) – it was not the devout pursuit of the laws of the Sharia that were the most important aim, but rather an internalized vision of God, a personal closeness to the supreme being. In extreme cases its aim is indeed a trance-like union with God is the aim, a state the Sufi tried to achieve with absolute faith, strict asceticism and quiet meditation. They also performed recitations of certain names and passages accompanied by rhythmic movements and other ecstatic rituals. However, their attitude, influenced not only by Christian monasticism but also by Hinduism, Buddhism and Agnosticism stands in contrast to orthodox Islam, and they thus encountered vociferous opposition right from the outset. Its detractors, however, were not able to prevent all mystics from preaching as admonishers and reforming priests over the centuries, and many of them were eventually revered as saints by followers during festivals and pilgrimages. That reverence continues to this day.

Inset, below: A desert road near Siwa, an oasis in the north-west of the country near the Egyptian border with Libya. The climate in this region is arid, with greater evaporation than rainfall.

Below: A limestone formation in the White Desert near Farafra, the smallest of four oases in the New Valley of the Western Desert. It was an important stopover for caravans back in Pharaonic times.

# WESTERN DESERT AND OASES

Kharga, Dakhla, Farafra, Bahariya and Siwa – these oases in the western reaches of Egypt, between the Nile and the border with Libya, are islands not only in the seemingly endless sea of sand but also in time. Recently, these remote outposts of civilization have been partially opened to visitors arriving by plane. Yet one gets the impression that the clocks still tick much more slowly here. There is no sign of stress anywhere. Perhaps that is why they are such a well-kept secret.

Shali, the Old Town neighborhood of Siwa Oasis, has a very unique charm. Below: The market square. Right: The remains of the Amun Temple, now known as the Temple of the Oracle, and a view of some old mud hut ruins.

## Siwa

The Siwa Oasis is more than 500 km (310 miles) west of the Nile and 300 km (188 miles) south of Marsa Matruh. Some 2,700 years ago, when Rome was but a village and Homer had only just completed his *Odyssey*, Siwa had already enjoyed great fame around the Mediterranean as the home of the powerful oracle to the mighty deity Amun-Ra. In 331 BC, Alexander the Great is said to have visited the Oracle to be confirmed the son of Amun and the rightful ruler of Egypt. In the 6th century BC, priests predicted death and doom for the Persian invader, Cambyses, who in turn sent his army into the Western Sahara to destroy all life in the Siwa Oasis. But the attackers vanished in a sandstorm before they were able to inflict any harm. Since then, the inhabitants of the oasis have believed themselves to be under the special protection of Amun-Ra.

Below: Narrow alleyways with traditional mud huts characterize the Old Town of El Qasr in the Dakhla Oasis cluster. Right: Wall frescoes and death masks decorated with gold leaf have been found in an ancient underground necropolis near the Bahariya Oasis.

## Dakhla, Farafra and Bahariya

The Dakhla Oasis served as a granary back in Roman times, and outside the main village of Mut the area has not lost any of its ancient fairy-tale charm. Aside from Balad, the "Village of Mud", one of the most attractive settlements here is El-Qasr (the Citadel), with narrow alleyways and palm frond roofs. Bahariya is also known for its extensive gardens and date palm groves. About halfway between here and Dakhla is Farafra, the small-est oasis in this cluster, which features a mud fortress ruin and idyllic palm garden set out in a fan shape around the village. In terms of travel, the village is a good starting point for excursions into the White Desert to the north, a dreamlike landscape dotted with snow-white limestone formations that could be straight out of a Dali painting. They have in fact been eroded by the elements over millions of years.

The colors and shapes of the desert are constantly changing, a beautiful metaphor for the ephemeral nature of life and the charm of new beginnings. For Antoine de Saint-Exupéry, the desert was "at once the most beautiful and saddest of the world's landscapes". Below: The Siwa Oasis. Right and insets below: The White Desert near the Farafra Oasis.

# THE COLORS AND SHAPES OF THE DESERT

On the seemingly endless narrow roads between the western oases you will discover the true meaning of the commonly used term a "sea of sand". The dunes that surround this vast sea are roughly 200 km (124 miles) wide and about 600 km (373 miles) long, and extend from the Qattara Depression all the way to the remote region where Libya, Egypt and the Sudan meet. It is here, between Djebel Uwainat and the Gilf Kebir Plateau, that Count László Almásy – the real "English patient" of cinema fame – went on his memorable expeditions. More importantly, it is also where, some 2,500 years ago, an army of 50,000 men disappeared without a trace beyond the expansive western horizon. They had been sent by the Persian King Cambyses to destroy the Siwa Oasis but were never seen again. Adventurers still search in vain for evidence of their fate. Among the most impressive features in the region are the limestone formations of the White Desert. Known locally as the "Mushrooms", they are a picturesque whim of nature that radiate in the most awe-inspiring range of colors, depending on the light. Amid the undeniable beauty here, however, it is important not to forget that the ubiquitous sands also represent a threat to monuments, agriculture and humans.

Below: The Hibis Temple, situated in a picturesque palm grove, was once dedicated to the deity Amun-Ra. Right, center: Traces of human life are quickly lost in the sand dunes between the oases of Kharga (far right) and Dakhla. Right: The El-Bagawat necropolis.

## Kharga

The southernmost oasis in the Western Sahara, Kharga, is home to more than 60,000 people, making it the largest as well. In the late 19th century, it was still an important station on the Darb el-Arbain, the "Forty Days Road", between Sudan and the Nile. Today it is the administrative center of the New Valley Province, comprising numerous autonomous villages such as Qasr Kharga, Bulaq and Baris. Some 30,000 ha (74,130 acres) of the oasis are used for agriculture, an amazing achievement since Kharga is regarded as one of the hottest places on Earth – the mercury can climb to 54°C in the shade and the sun shines an average of 4,400 hours per year. The best-preserved ancient sanctuary, the Temple of Hibis, dates from Persian times and was built around 500 BC. It is also worth seeing the early Christian necropolis of El-Bagawat.

"Belly dancing is first and foremost a harmonious union of music and the body," says "Lucy", one of the best-known belly dancers in Egypt. The tradition dates back to the days of the Pharaohs. Right, center: A depiction dating back to 1390 BC. Costumes are often adorned with coins.

# BELLY DANCING: A SUBTLE PRAYER TO EROS

You will rarely see them on the puritanical Arabian Peninsula, but in the more fun-loving Levant, including the Maghreb regions and particularly Egypt, belly dancers are often a standard element of an evening's entertainment. Many ancient Egyptian tombs contained illustrations of women who danced in front of the men –

primarily in the nude. Today, the more erotic zones are typically covered up, particularly when the spectators include members of a well-to-do wedding party, not an uncommon scenario. Conservative theologians from Al-Azhar University in Cairo condemn belly dance as "haram" – a sinful corruption of customs and morals.

Despite their vehement disapproval, however, Cairo (and Istanbul) is to belly dancing what New York is to jazz: the capital. For a novice, the body language may seem rather direct, especially a performance in the bars of Pyramid Road, Cairo's red-light district. Aficionados, on the other hand, regard belly dancing as a sublime prayer to

the god Eros, an art form rich in tradition and full of refinement that gets not just the hips and the ambience moving but also inspires the mind. For 30 years, Samia Gamal was the best-known belly dancer in Egypt. Today, dancers such as Lucy, Dina and Fifi Abdu, are thought of as her "granddaughters".

Inset, below: Sunset on the Nile between Dendera and Luxor. On its way through the Libyan and Nubian Deserts, the Nile has cut a valley 20 km (12 miles) wide and up to 300 m (1,000 ft) deep.

Hathor, the goddess of love, can be recognized by her headdress of cow's horns with a sun disc between them. These fine reliefs are in the Hathor Temple in Dendera, which is named after her.

# FROM EL FAIYÛM TO LUXOR

The stretch of the Nile from El Faiyûm to Luxor is about 500 km (310 miles) long and often overshadowed by the more famous sights of Upper Egypt. This may be due to the political conflicts between the Coptic population and radical Islamist forces, which frequently erupt in violence. And certainly, there are fewer monuments here of the same significance as those farther south. Nevertheless, a visit to the temples of Dendera and Abydos, or to the tombs in Beni Hasan is definitely worth recommending.

Facing page: View across the Nile Valley at El Minya. Far right: A sprawling "City of the Dead" south of El Minya. Right and below: With its magnificent wall frescoes, the necropolis of Beni Hasan is one of the most exciting archaeological finds in Central Egypt.

## El Minya, Beni Hasan

The provincial capital of El Minya, roughly 250 km (155 miles) south of Cairo, is a great base for excursions to the sights of Central Egypt. The main attraction, 20 km (12 miles) farther south, is the necropolis of Beni Hasan. It comprises thirty-nine rock tombs of "nomarchs" (governors) from the Middle Kingdom. Some of these contain beautiful wall paintings depicting scenes from everyday life or sporting activities. But the university town and bishops' see of El Minya itself also has some attractions: the shady manicured promenade along the Nile and the lively souk invite for a stroll, and the old villas from the days of the cotton boom are also worth seeing. Near the town of Sauiet el-Maitin, another 3 km (2 miles) south and accessible via the bridge over the Nile, is the largest necropolis in the country and is used by Muslims and Christians alike.

Facing page and below: Life on the Nile. Right: Before the Aswan Dam was built, the so-called "nilometers" measured water levels. Open shafts connected with the Nile by culverts had gauges at the center. Far right: A "tarbut", or wooden bucket wheel, used by the Fellahs.

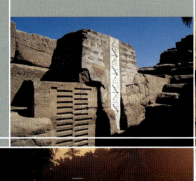

# MAN AND THE NILE: A FERTILE SYMBIOSIS

The fate of Egypt and its people has been inextricably linked with the Nile from the very beginning – and it will always remain so. The development of Egyptian culture would have been unthinkable without it. Its seasonal ebb and flow inspired ingenious technologies for diverting and damming the river depending on its changing levels; it triggered the evolution of advanced land surveillance methods; and it compelled the construction of canals and irrigation systems as far back as the first pharaohs. In order to determine the "tides" of the river in advance, Egyptians developed a calendar based on the heavens. Each year, the floods washed away most field markers, requiring the parcels to be measured anew and entered into land registers. Each year brought new quarrels, reminding each citizen of their duty to conform to the rule of law and obey governing authorities. And so the oldest organized political system of humankind after that of Babylonia was developed in Egypt, all under the influence of the Nile. Later, in the Old Kingdom, people used the Nile as a route for transporting people and granite from Aswan. It inspired them to build their imaginative sailing boats and ceremonial barges whose helms, rudders, hulls, masts and cabins were all used as models for future shipbuilders.

Copts have always been part of the Assiût community. Below and facing page: Sightings of the Virgin Mary have been reported at the Church of St Mark. Right: Unlike traditional Egyptian art, the archaeological finds of Tell el Amarna are characterized by an expressive realism.

# Assiût and
# Tell el Amarna

After his break with the priesthood of Thebes in the mid-14th century, Amenhotep IV made Tell el Amarna the new capital, halfway between today's cities of El Minya and Assiût about 15 km (9 miles) south-east of Mallawi. The ruler chose to elevate Aten, the ancient Egyptian sun god, to the position of solitary god. His name, Akhenaten, reflects the shift. Despite the fact that his successor, Tutankhamun, quickly returned the capital to Thebes, reversed the radical religious changes he made, and abandoned his magnificent palace, Akhenaten's concepts were ultimately a precursor of modern monotheism. Remains from his reign include important rock tombs with realistic depictions in the "Amarna style". In nearby Assiût, attractive villas along the Nile promenade and the Ibrahimiyah Canal are reminders of the cotton trade boom over a century ago.

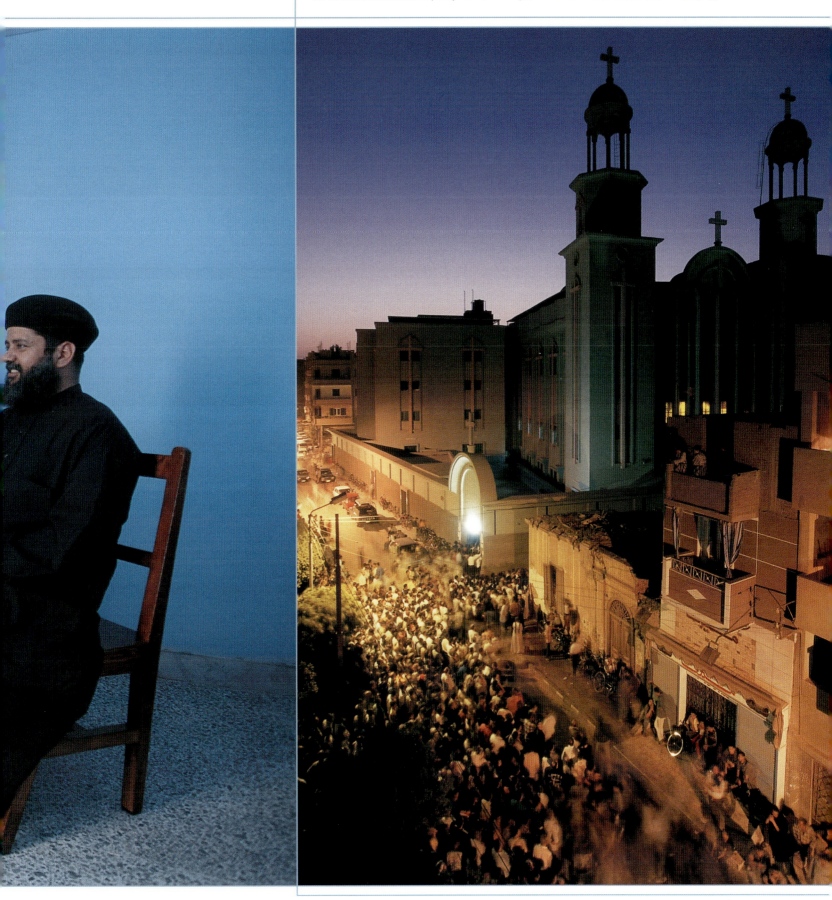

Below: The tombs, funerary temples and memorial stones in Abydos, the main sanctuary of the god Osiris, testify to the belief in the afterlife.
Right: The temple complex in Dendera was the most important place of worship for the goddess Hathor and her husband, Horus.

## Abydos, Dendera

The Dendera Temple complex, about 150 km (93 miles) north of Luxor, sits on the west bank of the Nile. The most recent of the great pharaonic sanctuaries, it is dedicated to Hathor, the goddess of love, and features a unique stone ceiling with gigantic architraves supported by twenty-four giant columns. The ceiling is decorated with a kaleidoscope of astronomical images and is well worth a detailed look. The magnificent reliefs in the interior chambers and a copy of the famous zodiac disc in the roof chapel also deserve a visit. Even more elaborate are the artistic features of the complex at Abydos (El-Âmirah), about 50 km (31 miles) south-east of Dendera. Osiris, the governor of the realm of the dead, is said to be buried here. Walls, ceilings and columns in the labyrinthine main temple are adorned with more than 600 large-scale illustrations.

Below: The Full Moon or Peace Festival at the Siwa Oasis lasts for three days. Inset, below: A wake-up call before Ramadan, the ninth month in the Islamic lunar calendar that is a month of fasting. Right: The Islamic calendar is lunar, based on the moon.

# THE LUNAR CALENDAR AND ISLAMIC FESTIVALS

The Islamic calendar is based on the lunar year, which consists of twelve months with twenty-nine or thirty days each. As a result, the alignment (or disalignment) of the Islamic and the Gregorian (Western) calendars shifts by eleven days each year. Over the course of thirty-three years, for example, festivals in the lunar calendar pass through all four seasons. Islamic computation of time begins with the first Muharram, July 15/16 of the year 622, when Mohammed and his followers migrated from Mecca to Medina. For a long time that date was used to calculate the years, but today the Western calendar is used in everyday life. The Muslim year has two canonical festivals: the breaking of the fast (in Arabic: Eid ul-Fitr) and the festival of sacrifice (Eid al-Adha). The former is a joyful expression of thanks to Allah for his support during the trying time of fasting. After communal prayers, people dress in their best clothes and spend time with friends and family as well as visit the graves of dead relatives. Presents are exchanged, old quarrels are settled and alms are given to the needy. Eid al-Adha, which commemorates God's forgiveness of Abraham, lasts for three days and includes the sacrifice of an animal if it can be afforded. It is a gesture of one's willingness to sacrifice in the name of Allah.

Inset: In ancient times, a road connected the temples of Karnak and Luxor, just less than 3 km (2 miles) apart. It was lined on both sides by sphinxes with the body of a lion and head of a ram.

Below: "See you on the terrace" – there is hardly a more stylish place to enjoy a glorious Egyptian sunset than on the terrace of the Old Cataract Hotel in Aswan. It has splendid views of the Nile.

# UPPER EGYPT

A cruise on the Nile in Upper Egypt reveals a seductively idyllic and consistent world – even if the ships do crowd the river between Luxor and Aswan in the high season. Children splash around; women tend to their washing; water buffaloes, ibises and the occasional camel graze the river banks; sand dunes and rocky cliffs mix with green sugarcane fields and date palm groves; the villages are dotted with mud huts and thatched roofs; and an array of funerary structures and temples completes the scene.

Today, only one obelisk adorns the entrance area of the temple complex in Luxor. The other one was shipped off to Paris in 1836 by Napoleon. In the 13th century BC, Ramses II had the complex enlarged with a giant tower (pylon). The statues in front of it depict the pharaoh.

## Luxor

Altogether, the small town of Luxor on the east bank of the Nile (with about 200,000 inhabitants), the temple town of Karnak, and the necropolis city of Thebes on the opposite bank of the river form a large cluster of ancient Egyptian cultural relics and are the main attractions for any journey to Upper Egypt. The foundation stone for the central temple complex, for example, which rises out of the middle of the urban area right on the promenade, was laid in about 1380 BC by Amenophis III (also known as Amenhotep III). A symbol of power in the New Kingdom, the temple was dedicated to the Thebes trinity of Amun, Mut and Chon. There are still a number of colossal statues, obelisks, pylons and papyrus columns spread out over 260 m (284 yd). The smaller artifacts from here and the other excavation sites are attractively displayed in the local museum.

Below: The pool at the Mena House in Cairo, built in 1869 for the inauguration of the Suez Canal, has a view of the pyramids. Right: The Winter Palace in Luxor opened in 1887. Center and far right: Agatha Christie drank tea at the Old Cataract Hotel in Aswan back in 1899.

# LEGENDARY HOTELS: WINTER PALACE, OLD CATARACT & OTHERS

Watching the sunset with a glass of champagne or a Karkadé rosehip tea on the terrace or by the pool at the Winter Palace Hotel in Luxor is an unforgettable experience for anyone cruising the Nile. The same can be said about the Old Cataract Hotel in Aswan, where Lawrence of Arabia recovered from his wild adventures and Agatha Christie thrashed out the novel *Death on the Nile* (1937) on her typewriter. Both of these legendary hotels fell into disrepair during President Nasser's days, but since then massive investment has returned them to their former glory. They now once again conjure up the sophisticated elegance of yesteryear and offer the high degree of comfort enjoyed in 1900 by the likes of pioneering travel agent Thomas Cook, who selected the hotel for his upscale clients on their classic "grand tours" of the Nile. Some similarly debonair establishments have withstood the ravages of time in the big cities. At the Mena House, outside of the city near the pyramids, for example, you can still get a glimpse of the old colonial styles, and the Cecil Hotel in Alexandria features elegant stucco, mahogany and lead crystal nuances. Unfortunately, the legendary Old Shepheard's Hotel, where "le tout Caïre" (all of Cairo) once gathered to take their afternoon tea, has long been demolished

In ancient Egypt, a temple was a likeness of the world, its columns symbolically supporting the firmament. The sanctum was hidden and even the king could only enter after observing strict purification rules. Below: The Great Hypostyle Hall in Karnak. Right: The temple complex.

## The Temple of Karnak

For several centuries, the temple complex at Karnak, north of Luxor, was Egypt's primary spiritual sanctuary. The temple was dedicated to Amun, the "Hidden One", a primeval deity who was mentioned in the pyramid texts of the Old Kingdom, but not made the imperial god of Thebes until 2000 BC, as Amun-Ra. The complex originally had ten entrance gates, so-called pylons, and the main entrance to the present compound of ruins leads through an alley lined with ram-headed sphinxes. One superlative follows another from here to the Precinct of Mut, more than 1 km (0.6 miles) away: the highest obelisk (30 m/98 ft, 323 tons), the Great Hypostyle Hall (134 petrified umbels and papyrus plants, each up to 10 m (33 ft) in circumference) and the most voluminous pylon at 113 m (371 ft) wide, 43 m (141 ft) high and 15 m (49 ft) thick.

Bottom, from left: The colossal reclining Ramses II in Memphis; the noble guardian before the former entrance to Luxor; and him on the sarcophagus that contained his mummy (right) when it was discovered in Deir el-Bahri in 1881. It is in the Egyptian Museum in Cairo now.

# RAMSES II: THE "PHARAOH OF PHARAOHS"

He had half a dozen principal wives, fathered ninety-two sons and 106 daughters, and died after sixty-seven years of rule, from 1301 until 1234 BC. He was nearly 100 years old. Indeed, Ramses II, son of Sethos I, did nothing by half-measures. His victory over the Hittites in the Battle of Kadesh was celebrated in one of the longest texts of ancient Egyptian literature. His cartouches can be seen carved onto the walls of a vast number of colossal structures, from the town of Tanis on the Nile Delta to Memphis and Luxor and into Nubia. Two anecdotes illustrate the charisma of this ruler from the 19th Dynasty still exercised even 3,200 years after his death: When Ramses' mummy was rediscovered in a grave robbers' hideout near the West Bank at Luxor and transported to Cairo by ship toward the end of the 19th century, thousands upon thousands of Fellahs lined the banks of the Nile filled with people wailing and prostrating themselves in reverence to their ancient ruler. And, in the year 1976, when the mummy – half-eaten by microbes and grubs – was sent to the Musée de l'Homme in Paris for professional restoration, the tradition-conscious French, who have a keen sense of proper etiquette, received the pharaoh at Charles de Gaulle airport with gun salutes and full military honors.

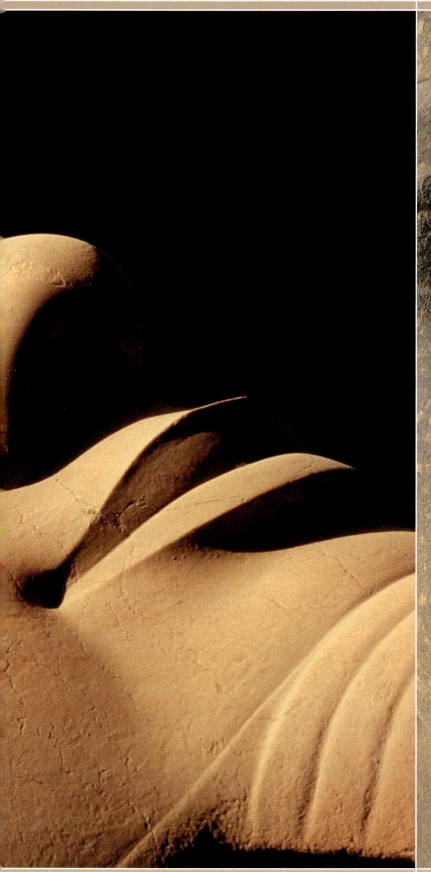

Hatshepsut was ancient Egypt's second female pharaoh. Below and inset: Her burial temple at the West Bank at Luxor. Right: The two Colossuses of Memnon are the emblem of the West Bank at Luxor. Far right: The burial temple of Ramses III (Medinet Habu).

## West Bank at Luxor

In the days of the pharaohs, the eastern bank of the Nile was the bank of life. Thebes, the "City of a Hundred Towers", as the Greeks called it, was where people settled and where the palaces and temples of the rulers were built. The West Bank, on the other hand, belonged to the deceased and was home to massive burial sanctuaries and necropolises. Among the multitude of temples, those of Ramses II (the Ramesseum), of Ramses III (Medinet Habu) and of Queen Hatshepsut (Deir el-Bahri) stand out. The latter, with its majestic ramps and terraces lined by pillars against the backdrop of a 300-m-high (985-ft) rock face counts as one of Upper Egypt's top attractions. Any visit should include a stop near the two Memnon Colossuses – seated statues measuring nearly 18 m (60 ft) in height built on orders from Amenhotep III.

Below: Tutankhamun rests in tomb no. 62, in a red quartzite sarcophagus in the Valley of the Kings. Facing page: The golden throne, a treasure from Tutankhamun's tomb, depicts the young pharaoh with his wife. Right: The Valley of the Kings was once known as the "Place of Truths".

## Valley of the Kings

In 1922, British archaeologist Howard Carter discovered the legendary treasures of Tutankhamun in the Valley of the Kings. So far, explorers have excavated more than sixty Pharaonic tombs in the sun-scorched rocky head of the valley at the northern outskirts of the West Bank in Luxor. But only about one-third of the tombs are accessible to the general public. A ticket gets you into three magnificent tombs where the walls are decorated with superb reliefs, some of them in astonishingly good condition. Measurements have shown that, during the high season, visitor hordes perspire up to 27 litres (6 gallons) a day in each chamber. It's no wonder then that the frescoes are rapidly fading despite many of them being encased in plate glass. The government has been forced to issue strict regulations to control the volume of visitors here.

Times may have changed since Howard Carter's discovery of Tutankhamun's tomb (right), but the amazement doesn't cease, regardless of whether it's in Abydos (below and facing page, center), in Dakhla (facing page, top) or in Alexandria Harbor (facing page, bottom).

# ARCHAEOLOGY PAST AND PRESENT

Computer tomography, a caesium magnetometer, a satellite camera, a laptop and an electronic microscope – archaeology has long since joined the high-tech age. In order to date stones and fabrics, reconstruct the design of buildings or detect underground buildings and structures, today's experts use methods their predecessors could not have dreamed of just two or three generations ago. It seems like light years since the pioneering days of Egyptology, when explorers like Bernardino Drovetti or Giovanni Battista Belzoni plundered the sites and transported shiploads of statues, obelisks, reliefs and other tomb treasures out of the country; or when Johann Ludwig Burckhardt discovered Abu Simbel, half-covered under the sand, and attempted in vain to excavate the site with his rudimentary tools. Even Howard Carter, who discovered Tutankhamun's tomb, would not believe his eyes if he saw the detailed study being carried out by Zawi Hawass, for example, at the settlement near the base of the pyramids of Giza; how Frank Goddio salvaged the remains of Ptolemaic palaces from the seabed in Alexandria's harbor; or the futuristic methods Kent Week employed in the Valley of the Kings to find the tombs of Ramses II and his sons, the largest Pharaonic burial site ever found.

To get inside the Edfu Temple, dedicated to the sun god Horus, you will have to pass the severe statue of Horus (facing page) in the shape of a falcon. Right: Only the ante-chamber of the Khnum Temple in Esna remains. Far right: The twin temple of Kom Ombo.

## Esna, Edfu, Kom Ombo

The three large temple complexes between Luxor and Aswan can be most easily visited on a Nile cruise. The first stop is the small town of Esna whose unfinished temple dates back to the Ptolemaic period. It is dedicated to Khnum, the ram-headed god who is supposed to have shaped humans from the mud of the Nile on a potter's wheel. An antechamber with 24 columns features depictions of Roman emperors in the style of the pharaohs. The Horus Temple of Edfu is still standing to this day, preserved exactly as it was built more than 2,300 years ago during the Ptolemaic Dynasty. Another architectural curiosity is the twin temple of Kom Ombo, also built in the Ptolemaic period. Arranged strictly symmetrically on its long axis, one half of the temple is dedicated to the falcon god Haroeris, while the other half honors the crocodile god Sobek.

Behind the walls of the dam, Aswan has developed into one of the most important industrial centers of Egypt and a lively, vibrant city whose markets (facing page) are also frequented by Fellah people (below) from the surrounding areas. Right: Inside the Nubian Museum.

## Aswan (1)

The final destination of a cruise into the south, and in fact the last major settlement in the country, is Aswan. In ancient times, this town, which now has more than half a million inhabitants, was the gateway to the African interior and an important trading center. Caravan routes from Nubia ended here and the ancient Egyptians began their military expeditions into the deep south from Aswan. The city was once named Yebu, land of the elephants. One theory says it was named after the place where Egyptians first encountered the pachyderms from the south; another asserts that it referred to the ivory that was once traded here and transported along the Nile all the way to the Mediterranean. The educational Nubian Museum offers a fascinating look into 7,000 years of civilization in the Nubian region to the south.

Bottom: A granite threshold divides the Nile and gives the area around Aswan its distinctive look. Right: Carrying water on the banks of the Nile. Facing page inset: The Isis Temple of Philae. It is said that Isis found the heart of her husband, Osiris, here.

## Aswan (2)

One of the most popular excursions in Aswan is a late afternoon cruise through the islands of the Cataract on a large-sail felucca. The heat of the day has subsided and the light softens to make the sand dunes look like golden honey. Enjoy some sweet tea on deck, and go ashore from time to time. On Kitchener Island, for example, you can stroll through the botanical garden before climbing the steep West Bank for a visit to the rock tombs of the nomarchs (local governors), the ruins of the Monastery of St Simeon, and the mausoleum of the Aga Khan – all situated high above the river with great views. You will also visit the Philae Temple of Isis and Trajan's Kiosk on the magical Agilkia Island and, a few miles farther along, the Kalabsha Temple, which was saved from the flooding cause by the Aswan High Dam.

Below: The Nubian village on Elephantine, a Nile island. Right: Lake Nasser, named after Egypt's former President, covers 5,250 sq km (2025 sq miles). A monument at its western end celebrates the friendship between the Egyptians and the Russians.

# Lake Nasser (Aswan High Dam), Elephantine

Near Aswan, the Nile is squeezed between granite rock formations, a fact that helped predestine the site for a dam. Between 1898 and 1912, British engineers built what would at the time be the world's largest reservoir. Around 1960, the Egyptians decided once again to harness the river's power, this time on a much larger scale and a bit farther south: the 3.6-km-long (2.3-miles) Sadd el-Ali Dam, completed in 1971 and 110 m (361 ft) high. During its construction, the soil that had to be shifted was ten times the volume of the Great Pyramid and some 120,000 Nubians had to be resettled. Today, you can meet the descendants of the "black pharaohs" on the Nile island of Elephantine, where time seems to have stood still in two of the villages. On the eastern side of Elephantine Island, it is worth visiting the ancient nilometer.

Thoth, the god of wisdom, is said to have devised the hieroglyphs (Greek for "holy characters"). Despite being pictorial (right) they form a logographic writing system that combined phonetics and semantics. With the help of the Rosetta Stone (facing page, right), it was possible to decipher hieroglyphs such as those on the sarcophagus from the Bahariya Oasis or in the Temple of Karnak (below).

# DECIPHERING THE HIEROGLYPHS

Two twists of fate occurred simultaneously in two places: In 1799, a French officer finds a stone in the coastal town of Rosetta that is engraved with a decree written in three different languages – Greek, Demiotic and Hieroglyphic. Then, in a faraway town in the South-West of France, a boy grows up with an unbelievable talent for ancient languages. Aged eleven, Jean-François Champollion is already fluent in Latin, Greek and Hebrew. Soon after that he takes on Arabic, Syrian, Chaldaic and Coptic, and becomes professor of history at the age of nineteen. When he sets his sights on deciphering the cryptic signs used by the ancient Egyptians, he pursues a theory that is completely contrary to that of his fellow linguistics colleagues. For him, the mysterious hieroglyphs are not symbols but letters. By comparing the texts on the stone from Rosetta, he can compile a trilingual list of the names of rulers, and on it he can decipher the names of Ramses and Thutmosis. He realizes that what had been written by the ancients since the days of the unification of the empire, around 3,000 BC, using rushes and ink on shards, papyrus or leather – or chiseled into a stone – was the equivalent of phonetic symbols (and thus syllables) and ideograms (and thus signs with a more complex meaning).

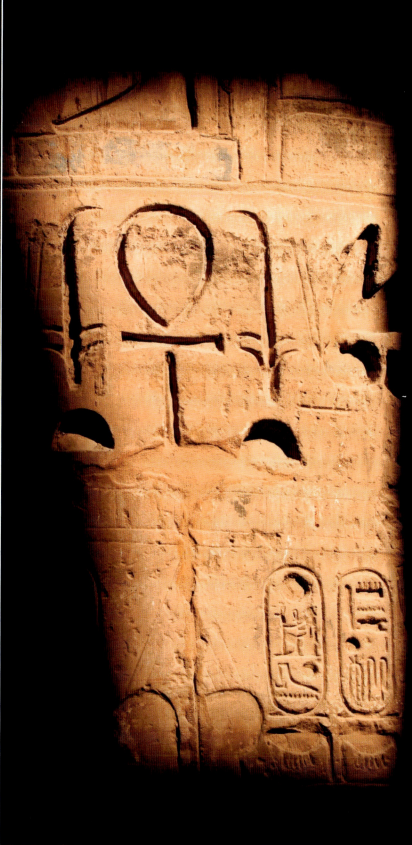

The Great Temple of Ramses II would have been submerged for eternity in the waters of Lake Nasser had it not been cut into blocks (of 20 tons each) and reassembled on higher ground. Right: Temple guardians with a key shaped like an "ankh", the ancient Egyptian symbol for life.

## Abu Simbel

The four colossal statues of Ramses II (20 m/66 ft) will without doubt be one of the lasting impressions from a journey along the Nile. The king had them sculpted in the 13th century BC on the West Bank of the Nile between the first and the second cataracts, at the narrow end of the temple dedicated to Amun-Ra and Re-Harakhte. No less impressive is the "small" Hathor Temple with its statues of Ramses II and his wife Nefertiti, each 10 m (33 ft) high. When the two gigantic temples were threatened by the newly constructed Nasser Reservoir, UNESCO had them transported to a location that was farther inland and 60 m (200 ft) higher. The project took four years. To pull it off, the cave temples were cut into more than 1,000 separate blocks, numbered, transported to their new position by flatbed trucks and reassembled.

Inset: Before construction of the Suez Canal, Lake Timsah was a swampy lagoon with brackish water. The situation has improved dramatically now that the canal flows through the lake.

Below: The Coloured Canyon, about 20 km (12 miles) north-west of Nuweiba, has been cut out of the limestone by the elements. Depending on the light, the rock takes on a wide range of red hues.

# SINAI AND RED SEA

The Sinai Peninsula is roughly 60,000-sq-km (23,000-sq-miles) in size and connects Asia with Africa. It is mostly featureless in the north, and throughout history has been a popular path of invasion for Egypt's enemies, from the Hyksos and the Persians to the British. Toward the south the landscape gets more dramatic, culminating in the spectacular area around St Katherine's Monastery at an elevation of 2,600 m (8,530 ft). The main draw, however, are of course the superb beaches and excellent diving sites on the Red Sea.

The lock-free Suez Canal was opened after only eleven years of construction. Insets below: The satellite picture shows the entire course of the canal; a logbook and naval map for the journey through the canal; the canal is illuminated at night for large container ships.

## Suez Canal

Around 20 million years ago, the Sinai Peninsula, the Arabian Peninsula and North Africa formed a single piece of land. Tectonic shifts later led these areas to break away from each other and form long gulfs on either side of the Sinai. The westerns side, the Gulf of Suez, is only about 95 m (312 ft) deep and separated from the Mediterranean by a landbridge that is only 160 km (100 miles) wide. It is said that Pharaoh Sesostris I had already dreamed of building a canal here, but his vision was not to be realized until the 1860s, by the Europeans. The detailed plan for the project was devised by the Austrian Alois von Negrelli, and the construction was managed by the Frenchman Ferdinand de Lesseps. After several interruptions caused by epidemics, political quarrels and financial crises, the inauguration was celebrated in the year 1869.

Below: The large harbor of Port Said – which is also the northern route into the Suez Canal – is protected by two mighty breakwaters, one of which juts far into the sea. Shown here is the Port Authority building. Right: Views of Ismailia, Suez, and Port Said.

ATALANTE

# Port Said, Ismailia, Suez

Of the three large cities along the Suez Canal, the town of Suez at the canal's southern end suffered the most serious damage during the Six Day War with Israel in 1967. Suez was largely rebuilt during the 1970s and today has more than 400,000 inhabitants, but a visit here is mostly defined by factory chimneys, harbor cranes and oil refineries. Nor do you need to allow too much time for a visit to Port Said. Considerably more charming is the town of Ismailia, founded in the year 1863 as a laborers' base camp during the construction of the canal. Located on Lake Timsah, it still possesses an attractive colonial district with beautiful villas, parks and boulevards, and it also boasts a vibrant Arabic quarter. The emblem of the city is the Port Authority administration building in the harbor, built in the Indo-Islamic style.

Right: A church door in St Anthony's Monastery depicts the two saints, Anthony and Paul, who decided to settle in this wild desert. Anthony was said to have realized only in a vision that a second hermit lived nearby, where the St Paul's Monastery stands today.

# Monastery of St Anthony

Named after St Anthony, the monastery was founded at the end of the fifth century and is considered the oldest hermitage in the Nile region. The 6-ha (15-acre), heavily fortified complex appears to have risen out of the desert and gives the impression of being impregnable. Its twin steeples can be seen from afar, surrounded by extreme solitude. The complex comprises, among other features, a church dating from the time of its founding, a 7th-century refectory as well as a valuable library, which is not open to visitors. Nearby, geographically separated from its fraternal monastery by a mountain range, the hermitage of St Paul of Thebes also features several ancient churches. It still encapsulates the spirit of a time when humans tested their souls in the desert (and not nuclear weapons) in an attempt to gain insight into the complexity of life.

Bottom: The fascinating mountain landscape around the Colored Canyon (inset). Right: Young Bedouins near Nuweiba; the pharaonic island near Taba with its fortress, built on orders from Saladin in the 12th century; a view of Dahab.

# Dahab, Nuweiba, Taba

The wide, meandering road takes visitors to the northeast from Sharm el-Sheikh through a rugged and beautiful mountain landscape. The peaks jostle each other with high, jagged ridges that go all the way down to the water. The coastal fringe is very narrow, with the exception of a few alluvial fans. Offshore is the strategically important island of Tiran, which creates a strait of only a few miles in the navigable channel to the Gulf of Aqaba, in the direction of Eilat. At the center of this swathe of land is Dahab. Its beaches and "Bedouin camps" are still reminiscent of the 1970s – hippies, pan flutes, dreadlocks, batik and psychedelia. Noticeably less laid-back, but with some high-end hotels, are the beach resorts of Nuweiba, 80 km (50 miles) farther north, and Taba, the last village before the Egyptian-Israeli border.

"... for the place on which you stand is sacred land". The Monastery of St Katherine, below, stands hidden behind fortress-like walls. Its most sacred building is the Chapel of the Burning Bush, built in 1216. It is named after the site where God revealed himself to Moses.

# Monastery of St Katherine

St Katherine's Monastery sits snug between the steep rock faces of the Wadi Araba, a plateau at 1,500 m (4,922 ft) elevation where it is said the Israelites once danced around the Golden Calf. At only 84 x 74 m (92 x 81 yds), St Katherine's is the smallest diocese in the world, and one of the oldest monasteries in all of Christendom. Its history stretches back to the year 330. It is said that at the time, the Byzantine Empress Helena and her husband Justinian were so impressed by the sanctity of this isolated spot that they had a small chapel built here. The monastery was only given its present name in the Middle Ages, following a rumor that the Greek Orthodox monks were keeping the corpse of St Katherine of Alexandria, the daughter of a Cypriot king, in their basilica. She is believed to have lived in Alexandria in about the year 300.

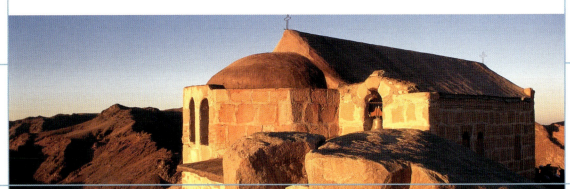

Below: View from Mount Sinai (Djebel Musa) where it is said, "They came to the desert of Sinai, and there Israel camped before the mount." Right: The chapel on the Mount is where Moses, leader of the Israelites, is said to have received the Ten Commandments.

## Mount Sinai

Approximately 50,000 people visit the Monastery of St Katherine each year. It is estimated that at least half of them climb the adjacent summit where, according to the Bible, Yahweh handed the prophet the Ten Commandments. Several routes lead to the top of Mount Sinai (2,285 m/7,497 ft), the most direct of which is via a stone staircase consisting of more than 3,000 steps. According to legend, the stairs were built by a single monk who was fulfilling a vow. The adjacent Mount St Katherine, at 2,637 m (8,652 ft) the highest peak of the Sinai, is climbed by considerably fewer people. Legend has it that an angel carried the bones of St Katherine of Alexandria to this peak, a story unknown until a hundred years after her execution. Uneven areas on the ground at the top of the summit are said to be imprints of her body.

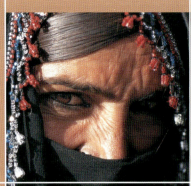

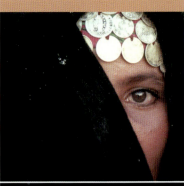

Bedouin women are very shy and immediately cover their faces when strangers approach. Their situation is difficult. They are revered and have a say in some matters, but are also discriminated against: Unlike men, they do not have the right to get divorces, nor are they allowed to remarry after their husband's death.

# ON THE ROAD IN BEDOUIN COUNTRY

In the second half of 1996, the region around the Monastery of St Catherine was declared a national park (since 2002, the land and the monastery have also both been listed as UNESCO World Heritage Sites). The protected area covers roughly 4,300 sq km (1,660 sq miles) and includes the mountain range of the southern Sinai, which is home to alpine ibexes, red foxes, striped hyenas, wolves and gazelles as well as 170 different species of medicinal plants. Some 7,000 Bedouins live here, albeit in a somewhat conflicted situation: the tourists riding camels, driving jeeps or going on guided tours through their native landscape brings a welcome income and a small degree of comfort to an otherwise extremely spartan lifestyle. Many are also taken on as seasonal workers in beach resorts, and during that time they swap their tents for a small concrete house. On the other hand, the Bedouins, whose women still wear colorful, full-length robes and the "gatif", a beautifully embroidered face veil, still wrangle regularly with the authorities, as do most of the Sinai's 120,000 or so semi-nomadic people. The government insists on demanding birth and marriage certificates, identity cards and, even worse, ownership registration for the land they have been living on and sharing for time immemorial.

Below: The Râs Muhammad National Park at the southern tip of the Sinai Peninsula protects a stunning area covering 480 sq km (185 sq miles) of desert and coastline. The park includes Tiran and Sanafir Islands, the sea around them and the coast at Sharm el-Sheik (right).

# Sharm el-Sheikh, Râs Muhammad National Park

Only one generation ago, Sharm el-Sheikh was still an insignificant fishing village. Now the southern tip of the Sinai has developed into a popular destination for sun worshippers and scuba divers. Infrastructure is concentrated essentially in two zones, the marina and Naama Bay, which has a natural sand beach fringed by a nice promenade. In addition, hoteliers have pledged not to exceed a maximum height of three storeys, to meet their own water requirements with the help of desalination plants, and to dispose of the wastewater in purification plants. The islands and most of the surrounding coastline – around Râs Muhammad as well as Nabq – are protected areas guarded by gamekeepers. And, indeed, the underwater world is an enticing option for water lovers. One session with a snorkel will convince just about anyone.

The Red Sea region's climate is warm-to-hot all year round and the water temperatures are pleasant – ideal conditions for a relaxing holiday. Below and facing page: Hurghada, a region fringed by beautiful lagoons, is very popular with divers (right).

# From Hurghada to Marsa Alam

In the early 1980s, there were only two hotels on the outskirts of Hurghada, a small fishing village on the western shores of the Red Sea about 400 km (250 miles) south of Suez. Today, that number has risen to more than 300, and the attraction to the region seems to be growing. That shouldn't be surprising, however, as all of the main factors for guaranteeing a successful beach holiday are available here in droves: sunny skies, crystal clear water, diverse fauna, and moderate temperatures all year round, both above and below water. The same is true for the nearby complexes in El-Gouna, Soma Bay and the Makadi Bay, built with the creature comforts of more upscale clientele in mind. Even more recent are the swimming and diving areas of Safaga and Quseir as well as Marsa Alam and Galeb farther south.

"The rainforests of the ocean", is what the reefs are sometimes called. The parallels are obvious: Like tropical rainforests, these sensitive underwater ecosystems possess the greatest biodiversity on Earth and, most significantly, are in need of special protection.

# AN UNDERWATER PARADISE

Besides its stunning mountain landscapes, the main attraction in the southern Sinai Peninsula is the sea. Divers from all over the world consider the reefs in the Gulf of Aqaba, between Sharm el-Sheikh and the border town of Taba, among the most appealing on the planet. Their proximity to the shore and the fact that they are quite shallow make them suitable for all levels of divers and snorkelers. The necessary infrastructure – from equipment hire to diving courses – is also readily available here. Roughly 250 types of coral and more than 1,000 fish species call this 1,500-km (932-miles) stretch of reefs home. The coral banks near Râs Muhammad on the southernmost tip of the peninsula are particularly splendid. In 1988, this area was declared Egypt's first national park. Over the last few decades, the west coast of the Red Sea has developed as another top destination for international diving tourism, thanks to resorts such as Hurghada, Safaga and Marsa Alam. This massive influx of tourism, however, has already caused noticeable damage to the ecosystem of the region. As a result, many sensitive species of fish have fled to less crowded stretches of the coast to escape the powerboats and schools of flailing humans. Unfortunately, the anchors from excursion boats have caused irreparable damage.

Traveling by taxi through Cairo you learn to be patient in the ubiquitous traffic chaos. "Es-sabr gameel" ("patience is beautiful") and "Insha' Allah" ("God wllling") are the mantras here.

# ATLAS

Geologically, Egypt consists mostly of rock, sand and mountainous desert on either side of the Nile Valley and the Sinai Peninsula. The climate is predominantly dry and hot, but in winter, temperatures can drop below 0 °C (32 °F) in the deserts and on the Sinai. The Mediterranean coast occasionally experiences heavy rainfall in winter as well. The Nile is the only major river in the country. The Red Sea and the Mediterranean are linked by the Suez Canal, one of the most important waterways in the world.

"Instead of traveling farther and farther, wouldn't it be better to travel slowly along the Nile? For it is no longer just a journey. It is life, a transformation, a dream of being ... and a truly profound reflection." (Rainer Maria Rilke)

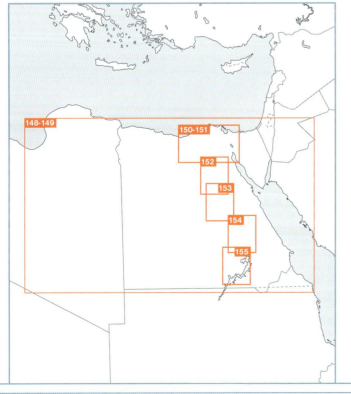

## MAP LEGEND
### 1:950,000

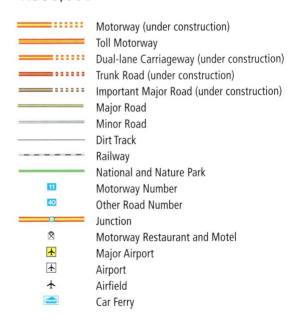

| | |
|---|---|
| | Motorway (under construction) |
| | Toll Motorway |
| | Dual-lane Carriageway (under construction) |
| | Trunk Road (under construction) |
| | Important Major Road (under construction) |
| | Major Road |
| | Minor Road |
| | Dirt Track |
| | Railway |
| | National and Nature Park |
| **11** | Motorway Number |
| **40** | Other Road Number |
| | Junction |
| | Motorway Restaurant and Motel |
| | Major Airport |
| | Airport |
| | Airfield |
| | Car Ferry |

# LEGEND

The maps on the following pages represent Egypt at a scale of 1:950,000. Topography and physical features are complemented by helpful indicators for travelers. For example, the road and transportation network is shown in great detail, and pictograms denote the location and type for the various points of interest and leisure destinations. Cities of interest to tourists are highlighted in yellow. The places that are listed as UNESCO World Heritage Sites are also listed.

## ICONS

**Renowned routes**
- Car Route
- Ship Route

**Natural landscapes and monuments**
- UNESCO World Natural Heritage Site
- Mountainous Landscape
- Rocky Landscape
- Gorge/Canyon
- River Landscape
- Lakeland Area
- Dune Landscape
- Depression
- Oasis
- Nature Park
- National Park (Landscape)
- Coastal Landscape
- Island
- Beach

- Coral Reef
- Protected Underwater Area
- Fossil Finds
- Wildlife Sanctuary

**Cultural monuments and events**
- UNESCO World Cultural Heritage Site
- Remarkable City
- Prehistory and Early History
- Prehistoric Rock Paintings
- Ancient Orient
- Ancient Egypt
- Ancient Egyptian Pyramids
- Greek Antiquity
- Roman Antiquity
- Nabataean Culture
- Islamic Cultural Site
- Jewish Cultural Site
- Christian Cultural Site

- Christian Monastery
- Historic Old Town
- Imposing Skyline
- Castle/Fortress/Fortifications
- Palace/Chateau
- Technical/Industrial Monument
- Dam
- Interesting Lighthouse
- Tomb
- Theater of War/Battle Field
- Monument
- Memorial
- Mirror and Radio Telescope
- Market
- Festivities and Festivals
- Museum
- Open-Air Museum
- Outstanding Building

**Sport and leisure destinations**
- Golfing
- Sailing
- Windsurfing
- Diving
- Swimming
- Seaport
- Leisure Park
- Viewpoint

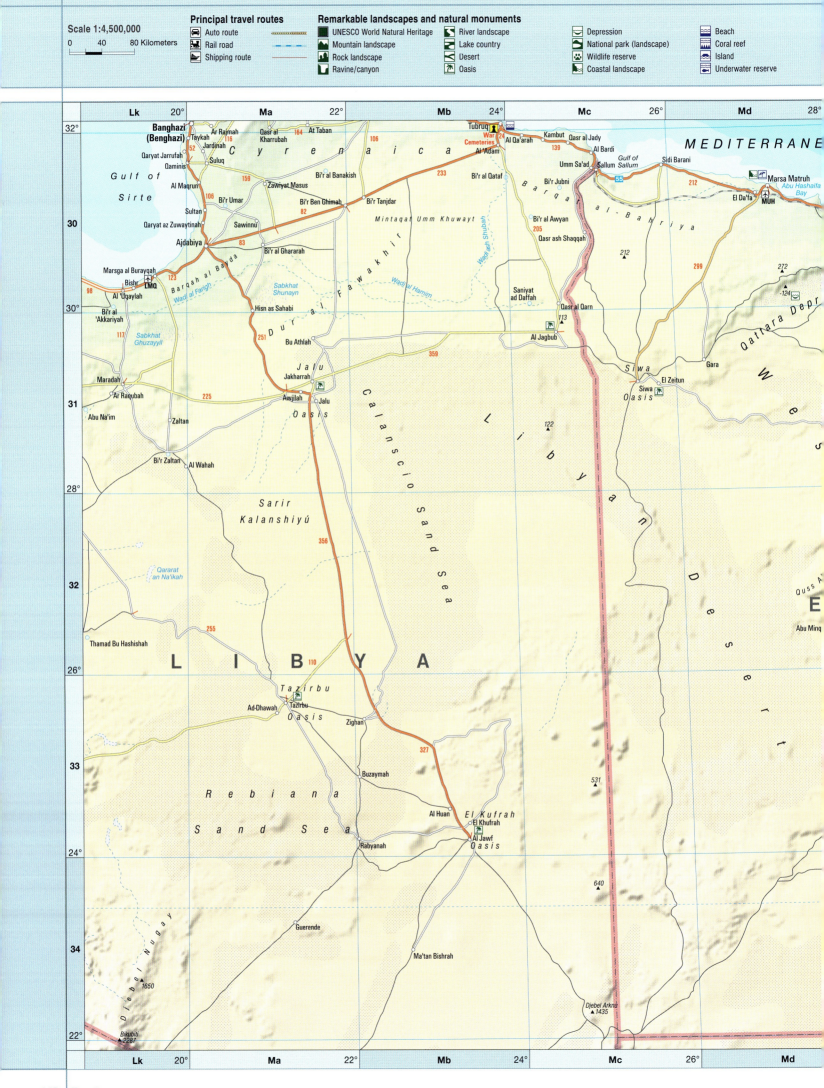

**Principal travel routes**

- Auto route
- Rail road
- Shipping route

**Remarkable landscapes and natural monuments**

- UNESCO World Natural Heritage
- Mountain landscape
- Rock landscape
- Ravine/canyon
- River landscape
- Lake country
- Desert
- Oasis
- Fossil site
- Nature park
- National park (landscape)
- Coastal landscape
- Beach
- Coral reef
- Island
- Underwater reserve

|  | Ad | Ba | Bb | Bc | Bd |
|---|---|---|---|---|---|

**01**

M E D I T E R R A N E A N

Rosetta Mouth
(Masabb Rashid)

Burg Migheizil

Lake Burul

63

N i l e

El Haddadi

13

Rashid
(Rosetta)

Abu Qir Bay

16    Idku    20

Idfina
El Aseifar

Fuwa

Mütûbis    Birriyet
El Aseifar    Sidi Sälim

Tida

Shalma

Canopus
El Mamoura

Abu Qir

Lake Idku

Deirut    El Mahmûdiya

Minshat Bulin

Kôm al Farä'in
(Buto)

Shabas
el Malh

Disûq    Shabas
el-Shuhadä

31

K S

El Montazah
Palace    38

EL ISKANDARIYA
(ALEXANDRIA)

Abu el-Abbäs Mosque

Pharos    Bibliotheca
Alexandrina

**SEA**

Graeco-
Roman
Museum

El Max

15

Alexandria    Kafr Silim
El Nhouza Airport

12

KAFR EL-
DAUWÂR

Birket Ghitas

Abu Hummus

El Mahmûdiya

El Rahmânîya

Shabas Imeir

El Bakatush

Ganag

Sais

21

Shubrä Khit

**02**

El Dikheila

Agami
Ezba Khamis

Lake
Maryut

21

24

6

Medinet el'Ameriya
el Guedida

El Baslaqun

Zawyet Sidi Ghâzi

34    Qafla

El Baleqtar

El Kom
el Akdar    Nideiba

Abu el
Matâmir    Hôsh Isa

37

DAMANHÛR

SUK

Farnawa

Ureln

Sä el-Hagar

Qaranshûr    Kafr
al-Zaiyât

Ityây el-Bärüd

Kôm
Hamâda

46

Ju'ay'l
(Naucratis)

El Dilingât

**03**

Gulf of Arab

(Taposiris Magna)
Abusir    65

Marakia

Marabella

Marina
El-Alamein

Porto Marina

El-Alamein

War Cemeteries
and Memorials

39

Borg el-Arab

Borg el-Arab el-Jadidah
(New Borg el-Arab)

Bahig

Kefret
Tâyil Müsa

Abu Mina

Bir ad
Qubayk

89

11

46

Ezba Isa
Hamad

Taftish Gianaclis

28

El Ghayata

El Kom
el Akdar

El Bamuqi

Saft el
Muluk

El Tod

Biban

El Yahudiya

Khirbita

Turat an Nubârîya

El Nubâriyah
el-Jadidah
(New Nobareia)

31

75

20

Wâdi Natrûn

Birkar al Ja'âr

Birkar
al Baydâ'

El Dahim

Wagid

Mudiryet
el Tahrin

Kôm Abu Billu
(Terenuthis)

11    30

El Khatâtibah

**04**

149

Djebel Khashm
el Qa'ûd

Dârat el Mashrûkah
-151

Djebel Hadid
185

Birkar
az Zuqm

Deir el-Baramûs

Umm Risha

Deir es-Surjân

Deir Amba Bshôi

Deir Abu
Makâr

SÂDÂT CITY

10

22

**05**

Qûr Laban
218

Birkar al Maghrûn

Bi'r Nähid

Wadi Al-Hitan
(Whale Valley)

Ghurd el Humayshât

Djebel Qantara
198

Djebel Ruzza
204

Qaret el Raml
200

Pyramids Gol

**06**

230

Djebel Gubr
182

Ghurd ar Tafasîkh

**07**

Ghurd Abu Samran

Ghurd ar Rammâk

Djebel Qatrâni

353

Qasr es

Medinet Dimai
(Soknopaios Nesos)

Dionysias

10

Lake Qârûn

-45

El Hammam

Qasr Qârûn
(Philoteris) Kôm Medinet Watifah

El Shawashna

Kalk

Abuksah

Sanh

|  | Ad | Ba | Bb | Bc | Bd |
|---|---|---|---|---|---|

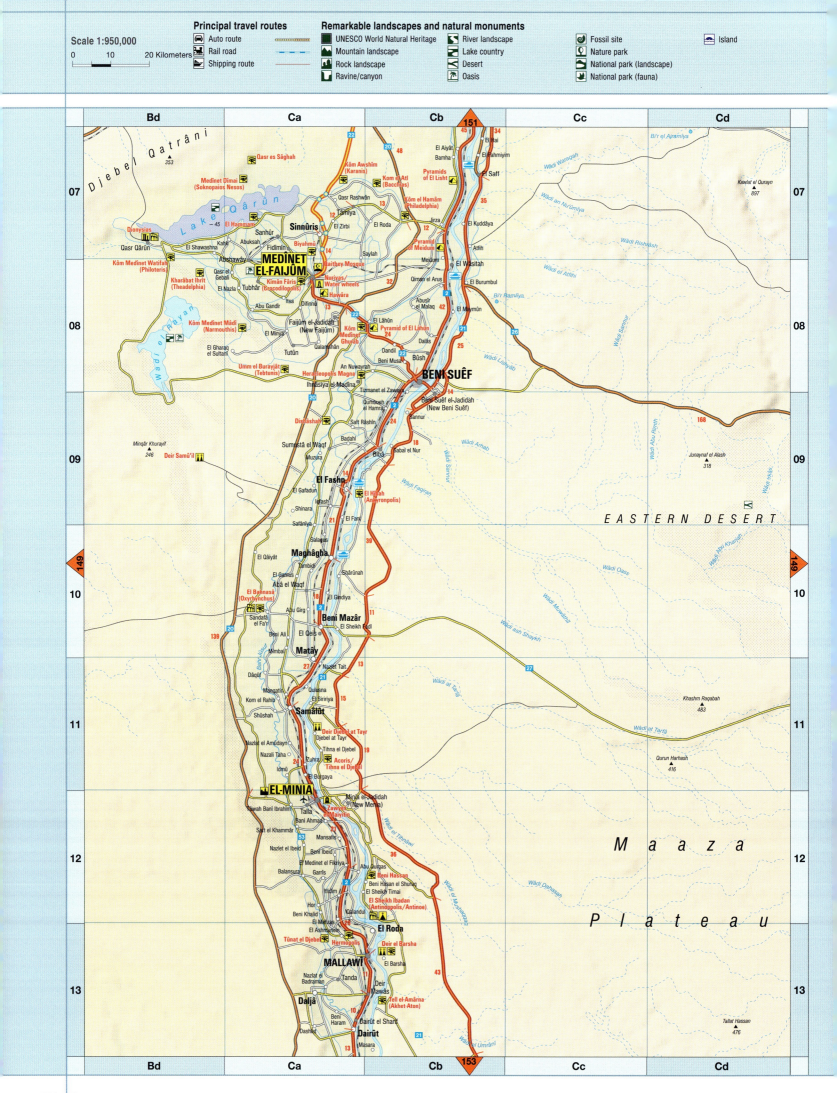

# Remarkable Cities and Cultural monuments

- ☐ UNESCO World Cultural Heritage
- 𓂀 Ancient Egypt
- 🏛 Ancient Egyptian pyramids
- 🏛 Greek antiquity
- 🏛 Roman antiquity
- ⛪ Places of Christian cultural interest
- ☪ Christian monastery
- ☪ Places of Islamic cultural interest
- 🏙 Historical city scape
- 🏰 Castle/fortress/fort
- 🏛 Palace
- 𓉔 Technical/industrial monument
- 𓉔 Dam
- ⬛ Tomb/grave
- 🏪 Market
- 🏛 Museum

## Sport and leisure destinations

- ⛳ Golf

Ca    Cb    152 Cc    Cd    Da

**Maaza Plateau**

*Nahr an Nil*

*Nile*

EL-MINIA
Minia el-Jadidah (New Menia)
Tûwah · Talla
Banî Ibrâhîm
Zâwyet el-Maiyitin
Banî Ahmad
Şurt el Khammar
Mansâfis
Nazlet el Ibeid
Banî Ibeid
El Medinet el Fikriya
Abu Jurqas
Balansura · Garis
Beni Hassan
Beni Hasan el Shurûq
Iflûm
El Sheikh Timai
Hor
El Sheikh Ibadan (Antinopolis/Antinoe)
Beni Khalid
Qalandul
El Manşara
El Ashmûnein
El Roda
Tûnat el Djebel
Hermopolis
Deir el Barsha
El Barsha

MALLAWÎ
Nazlat el Badraman
Tanda
Deir Mawâs
Dalğâ
Tell el-Amârna (Akhet-Aton)
Beni Haram
Dashlût
Dairût el Sharîf
Dairût
Masara
Sanabû
El Qusiya
Necropolis of Mir
Mir
Deir el Muharraq
Beni Rafi
Umm el Qusur
Beni Shiqeir
El Tatariya
El Ma'âbidah
Beni Sha'ran
Deir el Gabrâwi
Manfalût
Beni Muhammadiyât
Assiût el-Jadidah (New Assiût)
El Atamna
El Hawâtikah
Abnûb
Beni Adi
Masra
Arab Mutayr
Beni Zeid
El Izziya
Mangabad
ASSIÛT
Shutb
El Muti'a
Durunka
Convent of the Holy Virgin (Deir Durunka)
Mûshâ
Baqur
Beni Smei
Deir Tasa
El Zawiya
El Sahil
Abu Teeg
El Balayza
El Nikheila
El Badârî
El Zarobi
Sidfa
El Dîweir
Qâw el Kabîr (Antaeopolis)
Deir el Ganâdila
El Birba
El Itmaniya
Tima
El Nawâwra
El Ghanâ'im Bahrî
Umm Doma
Banga
Kôm Ishqaw (Aphroditopolis)
Tahtâ
El Khazindariya
El Tillhat
El Galawiya
Nazza
Ineibis
El Manâgha
Giheina
Fawqiya
Saquta
Tunis
Siflaq
Akhmîm el-Jadidah (New Akhmem)
Gezîret Shandawîl
El Salamuni
AKHMÎM
Deir el Ahmar (Red Monastery)
SOHÂG
Balasfûrah
Deir el Abyad (White Monastery)
Hawatim el Quseir
El Minshâh
Athribis
El Zuwek
El Kawamuil Bahari
Aulâd Ali
Aulâd Hamza
Sohâg el-Jadidah (New Sohâg)
Aulâd Yihya Bahari
Aulâd Salama
Naga el Deir
Bindar
GIRGÂ
Aulâd Toq Sharq
Beit Dawud Sahi
Minshât Bardis
El Kush
El Balyana
El Khiyam
El Haraga bil Qur'an
El Araba el Madfûnah
Abydos
El Tud
Samhud
Abu Tisht
Muwaslet el Wahah
El Kanak

*Wâdî el Tihnâwî · Wâdî el Muqatta'i · Wâdî Dahasah · Wâdî el Umrânî · Wâdî el Assiût · Wâdî Habib · Wâdî Abu Turayfiyan · Wâdî Sheydun*

Tallat Hassan ▲ 476
Kawlat el Farhîlah ▲ 487

*Melon Stones*

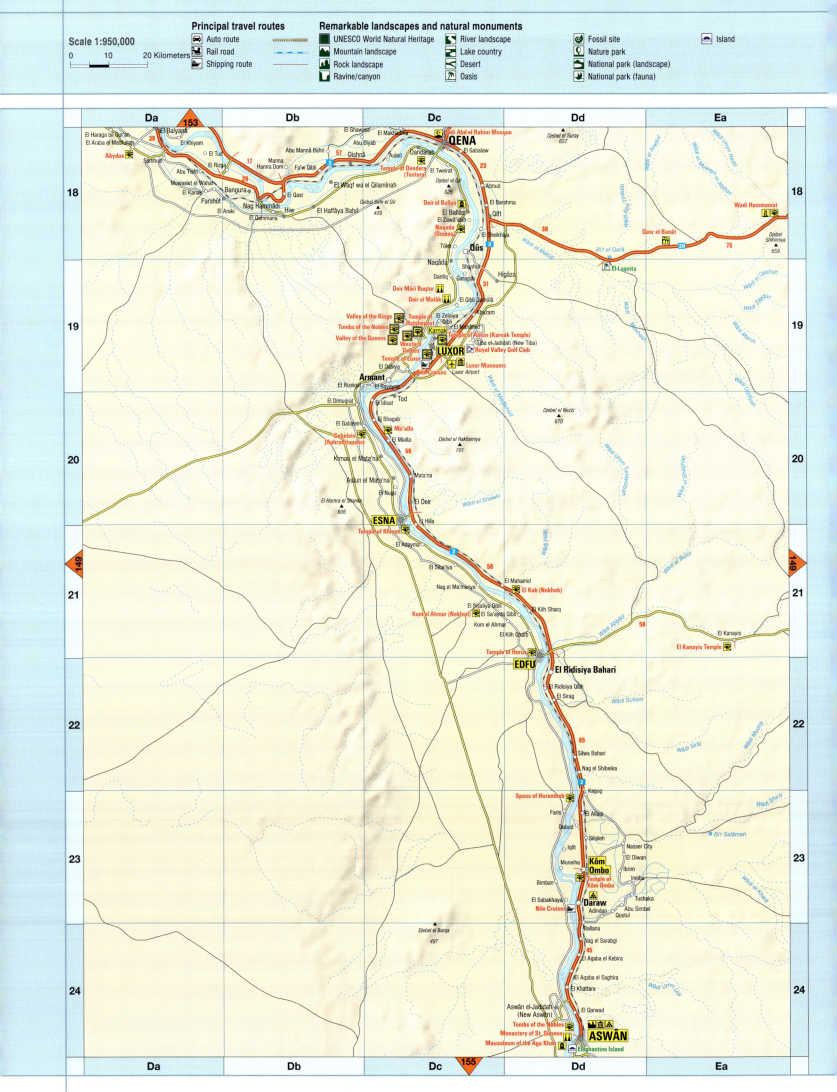

**Principal travel routes**

🚗 Auto route
🚂 Rail road
🚢 Shipping route

**Remarkable landscapes and natural monuments**

🟩 UNESCO World Natural Heritage
🔺 Mountain landscape
⬛ Rock landscape
📐 Ravine/canyon
〰 River landscape
🟦 Lake country
⬜ Desert
🌴 Oasis
🔷 Fossil site
🔶 Nature park
🌲 National park (landscape)
🦌 National park (fauna)
🏝 Island

**Da** · **Db** · **Dc** · **Dd** · **Ea**

153

El Haraga bil Qur'an
El Araba el Madfunah
**Abydos**
El Balyana
38
Sohag
El Khiyam
El Tud
El Rizqa
Manna
Hamra Dom
Abu Diyab
Fa'w Qibli
El Ghawasa
El Makhadma
**QENA**
Sidi Abd-el Rahim Mosque
El Gabalaw
57
Dishnâ
Aulad
**Dandarah**
**Temple of Dendera (Tentyra)**
El Tweirat
23
Djebel el Suray 657
El Ghushi
Abnud
Wadi Hammamat
A
Abu Tisht
Muwaslet el Wahat
El Kanak
Bangura
29
El Qasr
Nag Hammâdi
El Araki
El Qammana
Hiw
El Halfâya Bahri
Farshût
El Waqf wa el Qilamînah
Djebel Sirin el Gir 409
Djebel el Gir 526
Deir el Ballas
El Ballâs
El Zawâ'idah
**Naqâda (Ombos)**
El Sheikhila
Qift
38
Qasr el Banât
Djebel Shihimiya 659
75
29
**18**
**Dûs**
Naqâda
Shanhûr
Garagûs
Higâza
Danfiq
El Lageita
31
Deir Mâri Buqtur
Deir el Malâk
El Qibli Qamûla
Khûzam
**19**
El Zelniya
Qibli
El Mahamid
**Valley of the Kings**
**Temple of Hatshepsut**
**Tombs of the Nobles**
**Karnak**
**Temple of Amun (Karnak Temple)**
**Valley of the Queens**
Tiba el-Jadîdah (New Tiba)
**Western Thebes**
**Royal Valley Golf Club**
**LUXOR**
**Temple of Luxor**
El Dabiya
**Nile Cruises**
Luxor Airport
Luxor Museums
**Armant**
El Rayayna
El Rizeiqat
Tod
El Idisat
El Dimuqrat
El Shagab
El Gabelein
**Mo'alla**
**Gebelein (Aphroditopolis)**
El Mialla
Djebel el Nezzi 670
**20**
Kiman el Mata'na
56
Djebel el Rakhamiya 701
Astun el Mata'na
Mata'na
El Nugu
El Deir
El Homra el Shanka 606
El Hilla
Wâdi el Shawki
**ESNA**
**Temple of Khnum**
El Adayma
2
**149**
El Siba'iya
56
**21**
Nag el Ma'mariya
El Mahamid
**El Kab (Nekheb)**
El Bisaliya Qibli
El Kilh Sharq
**Kom el Ahmar (Nekhen)**
El Sa'ayda Qibli
Kom el Ahmar
El Kilh Gharb
El Kanayis
**Temple of Horus**
58
**El Kanayis Temple**
**EDFU**
**El Ridisiya Bahari**
El Ridisiya Qibli
El Sirag
**22**
65
Silwa Bahari
Nag el Shibeika
**Speos of Horemheb**
2
Kagug
Faris
El Allaqi
Dabud
Djebel el Barqa 497
Iqlit
Silsileh
Nasser City
El Diwan
**23**
Muneiha
Ibrim
**Kôm Ombo**
**Temple of Kôm Ombo**
Bimban
Ineiba
El Sabakhaya
Adindan
**Daraw**
Abu Simbel
**Nile Cruises**
Qustul
Ballana
Tushaka
Nag el Sarabgi
45
El Aqaba el Kebira
**24**
El Aqaba el Saghira
Wâdi Umm Ugl
El Khattara
Aswân el-Jadîdah (New Aswan)
El Qarwad
**Tombs of the Nobles**
**Monastery of St. Simeon**
**ASWÂN**
**Mausoleum of the Aga Khan**
Elephantine Island
155

**Da** · **Db** · **Dc** · **Dd** · **Ea**

## Remarkable Cities and Cultural monuments

- ☐ UNESCO World Cultural Heritage
- ⚐ Ancient Egypt
- ⚐ Ancient Egyptian pyramids
- ⚎ Greek antiquity
- ⚐ Roman antiquity
- ⚐ Places of Christian cultural interest
- ⚐ Christian monastery
- ☪ Places of Islamic cultural interest
- ⚎ Historical city scape
- ⚐ Castle/fortress/fort
- ⚐ Palace
- ⚐ Technical/industrial monument
- ⚐ Dam
- ⚐ Tomb/grave
- ⚐ Market
- ⚎ Museum

## Sport and leisure destinations

- ⚐ Golf

**154** (Db)

**149** (Cd/Dd)

Djebel el Barqa
497

Nag el Sarabgi
**45**
El Aqaba el Kebira
El Aqaba el Saghira
El Khattara

Aswân el-Jadidah
(New Aswân)
El Qarwad

**Tombs of the Nobles**
**Monastery of St. Simeon**
**Mausoleum of the Aga Khan**
**ASWÂN**

572

**First Cataract**
**Aswân Low Dam**
**Elephantine Island**
**Temple of Philae**

Medinet Sahara
(Sahara City)
**Sadd el Ali/**
**Aswân High Dam**

Aswân - Daraw Airport
**Kalabsha Temple**
**(Kalabsha Island)**

Kurkur

367

467

**L a k e**

**N a s s e r**

Dunqul

*S i n n   e l   K a d d â b*

**149**

*Toshka*
*Lakes*

305

**Toshka Project** ⚐
**(Southern Valley Development Project)**
**(under construction)**

**(Temple of Wadi el-Sebua)**
**El Sibu Temple**

**Dakka Temple**

**Amada Temple**

Sheikh Zayed Canal ⚐

396

**Mubarak** ⚐
**Pumping Station**

**Qasr Ibrim**

353

323

**Abu Simbel**

**149** (Db)

The index listings refer to the section of the picture and the maps. After the key word is a pictogram that refers to the point of interest according to the map entry (see pg. 147). The page number and key word entry for the map section are in bold. After that is the page number for the picture and finally there are Internet addresses where you can quickly find current information about the locations and sights mentioned in this volume. Most of the entries on the image pages are also in the maps, which give you additional helpful travel information.

From left: At the pyramids of Giza; the Old Town of El Qasr in Dakhla Oasis; a view of Mount Sinai; Elephantine, an island on the Nile; Coptic mass in Cairo.

## Picture Credits

Abbreviations:

A      Alamy
C      Corbis
CE    Clemens Emmler
G      Getty
L      Laif
MM    Michael Martin
P      Premium

t = top, b = bottom, c = center, l = left, r = right

Pictures listed in clockwise order starting at the top left

S. 1 CE, 2/3 G/Photographer's Choice/Sylvain Grandadam 4/5 CE, 6/7 CE, 8 L/Emmler, 8/9 L/Krause, 10.1 akg-images/Erich Lessing, 10.2 akg-images/Werner Forman, 10.3 akg-images/Erich Lessing, 10.4 akg-images/ Werner Forman, 10/11 Hervé Champollion/ akg-images, 11.1 akg-images/Werner Forman, 11.2 akg-images/Rabatti-Domingie, 11.3 akg-images/Hervé Champollion, 11.4 akg-images/ Hervé Champollion, 12 tl L/ Heeb, 12 tr L/Heeb, 12/13 L/Emmler, 13 CE, 13.1 L/Hemispheres, 14 CE, 14/15, 14 tl L/ Heeb, 14 oM L/Krause, 14 tr L/Krause, 14/15 L/Heeb, 15 t L/Hemispheres, 15 M L/Emmler, 15 b L/Heeb, 16 tl akg-images/ Hilbich, 16 oM L/Gamma, 16 tr L/Krause, 16/17 L/Krause, 17 L/Tatlow, 18 t L/Krause, 18.1 G/Stone/NPA, 18.2 CE, 18/19 L/Krause, 20 tl CE, 20 oM CE, 20 tr CE, 20.1 CE, 20.2 MM, 20.3 CE, 20.4 CE, 21 CE, 22 tl C/ Roger Wood, 22 oM C/Sandro Vannini, 22 tr C/Roger Wood, 22.1–5 L/Gamma, 23.1–4 L/Gamma, 23.2 L/Gamma, 24 tl L/Krause, 24 oM L/Krause, 24 tr L/Krause, 24 L/Krause,

25. 1 L/Krause, 25.2 L/Krause, 25.3 L/Krause, 25.4 C/K. M. Westermann, 26 tl C/Dave Bartruff, 26 tr C/Dave Bartruf, 26/ C/Andrea Jemolo, 27 o. ifa/W. Grubbe, 27 M A/Eddie Gerald, 27 b A/Peter Jousiffe, 28 tl L/VU, 28 oM P/Buff, 28 tr L/Gamma, 21.1 L/Krause, 28.2 L/Krause, 28.3 L/Emmler, 28.4 CE, 28.5 CE, 28/29 L/Krause, 30 tl CE, 30 tr CE, 30 C/Carmen Redondo, 30/31 C/Carmen Redondo, 32 L/Heeb, 32/33 CE, 34 t L/Heeb, 34/35 L/Krause, 35 CE, 36 t CE, 36 CE, 36/37 L/Emmler, 38 tl L/Kirchgessner, 38 M L/Emmler, 38 tr L/Krause, 31.1 L/Kirchgessner, 38.2 L/Krause, 39.1 L/Laif, 39.2 CE, 40 tl L/Emmler, 40 oM L/Emmler, 40 tr L/Emmler, 40/41 L/Krause, 41 t L/Klrchgessner, 41 M L/Emmler, 41 b L/Heeb, 42 tl L/Kirchgessner, 53 oM CE, 42 tr L/Emmler, 42/43 L/Emmler, 43 L/Emmler, 44 tl CE, 44 tr CE, 44/45 CE, 46 t CE, 46/47 L/CE, 48 o. akgimages/Andrea Jemolo, 48 A/Gordon Sinclair, 48/49 A/Gordon Sinclair, 49 A/Gordon Sinclair, 50 tl L/Emmler, 50 tr CE, 50.1 L/CE, 50.2 A/Eddie Gerald, 50/51 L/Kirchgessner, 52 tl L/Kimmig, 52 oM L/Kirchgessner, 52 tr C/Reuters/Victoria Hazou, 52.1 A/John Wreford, 52/53 CE, 54 tl CE, 54 tr CE, 54/55 MM, 55 t CE, 55 M CE, 55 b L/CE, 56 P/Janek, 56/57 P, 58 tl L/Heeb, 58 oM L/Emmler, 58 tr L/Emmler, 58/59 CE, 59 CE, 60 tl Ifa/ArnoldImages, 60 oM CE, 60 tr L/Krause, 60/61 CE, 62 tl G/The Bridgeman Art Library, 62 oM G/The Bridgeman Art Library, 62/or C/Christie's Images, 62/63 G/The Bridgeman Art Library, 63 G/The Bridgeman Art Library, 64 t CE, 64/65 L/Krause, 65 L/Gamma, 66 tl L/Krause, 66 oM L/Emmler, 66 tr L/Krause, 66/67 L/Krause, 68 t L/Kirchgessner, 68 G/Frans Lemmens, 69 L/Hemispheres, 70 G/Panoramic Images, 70/71 CE, 72 tl L/Emmler, 72 tr CE, 72/73 L/Emmler, 74

tl L/Emmler, 74 tr L/Emmler, 74 L/Fechner, 74/75 CE, 76 tl L/Hemispheres, 76 tr L/Gamma, 76 bl mauritius images/Richard Mayer, 76 br mauritius images/Frank Lukassek, 76/77 G/Image Bank/ Sylvain Grandadam, 78 tl Bildarchiv Monheim/ Rainer Kiedrowski, 78 oM A/ Robert Harding Picture Library Ltd, 78 tr L/Emmler, 78 L/Emmler, 78/79 CE, 80 tl CE, 80 oM L/Laif, 80 tr CE, 80 CE, 80/81 L/Emmler, 82 A/Helene Rogers, 82/83 A/ BL Images Ltd, 84 tl C/Sandro Vannini, 84 tr C/zefa/Theo Allofs, 84.1 C/Sandro Vannini, 84.2 C/Sandro Vannini, 84.3 C/ Gianni Dagli Orti, 84/85 C/Sandro Vannini, 86 tl MM, 86 tr L/Emmler, 86 tr MM, 86.1–3 MM, 86/87 MM, 88.1 C/Francis G. Mayer, 88.2 C/Ruggero Vanni, 88.3 C/Sandro Vannini, 88.4 C/The Art Archive, 88.5 akg-images/Werner Forman, 86 L/Krause, 87/87 L/Krause, 87 L/Krause, 90 tl C/Wolfgang Kaehler, 90 oM f1 online, 90 tr C/Wolfgang Kaehler, 90.1 C/Sandro Vannini, 90.2 C/Roger Wood, 90.3 C/Roger Wood, 91.1 C/Roger Wood, 91.2 C/Robert Holmes, 91.3 C/Roger Wood, 92 tl A/Eyebyte, 92 tr A/Chad Ehlers, 92 L/Krause, 92/93 L/Krause, 94 L/Emmler, 94/95 L/ Hemispheres, 96 t L/ Arthur Selbach, 96 G/Westmoreland, 96/97 L/Krause, 97 t Mediacolor's, 97 M CE, 97 b DFA/Riedmiller, 98 tl L/LITTAYE ALAIN, 98 oM CE, 98 tr CE, 98/99 L/Heeb, 100 t L/Heeb, 100 b IFA-Bilderteam/Alexandre, 100/101 MM, 102 t G/National Geographic/ Kenneth Garrett, 102/103 C/Christophe Boisvieux, 102 l L/Krause, 103 r akg-images, 104 tl P/Nawrocki/Stock/S. Vidler, 104 tr C/Tibor Bognár, 104 MM, 104/105 P/T. Smith, 106 tl MM, 106 tr MM, 106/107 P, 107 Hub/Damm 108 tl C/Hulton-Deutsch Collection, 108 oM C/Hulton-Deutsch Collection, 108 tr C/Bettman, 108/109

G/National Geographic, 109 t A/Bennett-Photo, 109 M G/ National Geographic, 109 b Franck Goddio/Hilti Foudation (Foto: Christoph Gerigk), 110 tl A/Elvele Images, 110 tr MM, 110 L/Krause, 110/111 MM, 111 L/Krause, 112 tl L/Krause, 112 tr L/Modrow, 112/113 MM, 113 t MM, 113 Mitte links CE, 113 Mitte rechts CE, 113 b L/Emmler, 114 t MM, 114/115 Hub/Zoom 115 stone_press, 116 tl MM, 116 oM MM, 116 tr CE, 116 L/Emmler, 117 L/Emmler, 118.1 G/Riser, 118.2 G/National Geograhic, 118.3 G/Taxi, 118.4 C/Bettmann, 118/119 G/National Geographic, 119 L/Modrow, 120 tl L/Hemispheres, 120 oM L/Krause, 120 tr L/Krause, 120.1 P/Boyer, 120.2 G, 120/121 Hub, 122 L/Emmler, 122/123 L/Kirchner 124 t ifa-bilderteam/Picture Finders, 124.1 C/NASA, 124.2 L/Krause, 124.3 L/Krause, 124/125 L/Krause, 126 tl A/Eddie Gerald, 126 oM A/KHALED KASSEM, 126/127 L/Emmler, 128 tl L/Emmler, 128 oM CE, 128 tr CE, 128/139 CE, 130 tl L/Kirchgessner, 130 oM A/Robert Harding Picture Library Ltd, 130 tr A/Jon Arnold Images, 130/131 A/Jon Arnold Images, 131 L/Martin Kirchner, 132 tl MM, 132 oM CE, 132 tr L/Krause, 132/133 MM, 134 t L/Kirchner, 134/135 L/Kirchner, 136 tl L/Emmler, 136 oM CE, 136 tr C/Kevin Fleming, 136/137 CE, 138 t A/DAVID NOBLE PHOTOGRAPHY, 138.1 CE, 138.2 CE, 138/ 139 CE, 140 tl SAS/Alamy, 140 oM SAS/ Alamy, 140 tr LOOK-foto/Reinhard Dirscherl, 140/141 mauritius images/Josef Beck, 141 mauritius images/Peter Lehner, 142 tl L/Hemispheres, 142 oM L/RAPHO, 142 tr L/Hemispheres, 142/143 L/Hemispheres, 143.1–10 L, 144/ 145 L/Kirchgessner, 146/ 147 L/Emmler, 159 L/Emmler

This edition is published on behalf of APA Publications GmbH & Co. Verlag KG, Singapore Branch, Singapore by Verlag Wolfgang Kunth GmbH & Co KG, Munich, Germany

Distribution of this edition:

**GeoCenter International Ltd**
**Meridian House, Churchill Way West**
**Basingstoke, Hampshire RG21 6YR**
**Great Britain**
**Tel.: (44) 1256 817 987**
**Fax: (44) 1256 817 988**
**sales@geocenter.co.uk**
**www.insightguides.com**

ISBN 978-981-282-003-7

Original edition:
© 2008 Verlag Wolfgang Kunth GmbH & Co. KG, Munich
Königinstr. 11
80539 Munich
Ph: +49.89.45 80 20-0
Fax: +49.89.45 80 20-21
www.kunth-verlag.de

English edition:
Copyright © 2008 Verlag Wolfgang Kunth GmbH & Co. KG
© Cartography: GeoGraphic Publishers GmbH & Co. KG

Text: Walter M. Weiss
Translation: Sylvia Goulding
Editor: Kevin White for bookwise Medienproduktion GmbH, Munich
Production: bookwise Medienproduktion GmbH, Munich

Printed in Slovakia

The information and facts presented in this book have been extensively researched and edited for accuracy. The publishers, authors, and editors, cannot, however, guarantee that all of the information in the book is entirely accurate or up to date at the time of publication. The publishers are grateful for any suggestions or corrections that would improve the content of this book.